BY LINDSEY CARMAN

The Young Adult's Guide to Flawless Writing

Essential Explanations, Examples, and Exercises

The Young Adult's Guide to Flawless Writing: Essential Explanations, Examples, and Exercises

Copyright © 2016 by Atlantic Publishing Group, Inc.
1405 SW 6th Ave. • Ocala, Florida 34471 • 800-814-1132 • 352-622-1875–Fax
Web site: www.atlantic-pub.com • E-mail: sales@atlantic-pub.com
SAN Number: 268-1250

Library of Congress Cataloging-in-Publication Data

Names: Carman, Lindsey, 1992-
Title: The young adult's guide to flawless writing : essential explanations,
    examples, and exercises / by Lindsey Carman.
Description: Ocala, Florida : Atlantic Publishing Group, 2015.
Identifiers: LCCN 2015033289 | ISBN 9781601389817
Subjects: LCSH: Composition (Language arts) | English language--Composition
    and exercises--Study and teaching (Higher).
Classification: LCC LB1631 .C393 2015 | DDC 808/.0420712--dc23 LC record available at
http://lccn.loc.gov/2015033289

Printed on Recycled Paper

Printed in the United States

Reduce. Reuse.
RECYCLE.

A decade ago, Atlantic Publishing signed the Green Press Initiative. These guidelines promote environmentally friendly practices, such as using recycled stock and vegetable-based inks, avoiding waste, choosing energy-efficient resources, and promoting a no-pulping policy. We now use 100-percent recycled stock on all our books. The results: in one year, switching to post-consumer recycled stock saved 24 mature trees, 5,000 gallons of water, the equivalent of the total energy used for one home in a year, and the equivalent of the greenhouse gases from one car driven for a year.

Over the years, we have adopted a number of dogs from rescues and shelters. First there was Bear and after he passed, Ginger and Scout. Now, we have Kira, another rescue. They have brought immense joy and love into not just into our lives, but into the lives of all who met them.

We want you to know a portion of the profits of this book will be donated in Bear, Ginger and Scout's memory to local animal shelters, parks, conservation organizations, and other individuals and nonprofit organizations in need of assistance.

– Douglas & Sherri Brown,
President & Vice-President of Atlantic Publishing

Dedication

Mom and Dad, your supportive encouragement
and love have formed who I am today.

Roger, you're the light that helps me find my
way. Thanks for doing life with me.

TABLE OF CONTENTS

FOREWORD

The art of writing is hard to master; even the literary greats can tell you that. Becoming a great writer takes time, practice and dedication. So when you struggle with writing essays for college admissions, let alone get a handle on correct grammar, it may seem like  you'll never be able to write as well as you would like to. Have no fear—it's never too late to learn correct grammar and write eloquent sentences, especially if you're still in high school.

Whether you want to become the next J.K. Rowling or follow in the steps of Mark Zuckerberg, you *need* to know how to write well. Writing is a necessary function for communication, especially in the business world. From typing up brief emails to writing project reports to creating a thesis for research, the art of writing is needed in almost every aspect of life—there's no way of escaping it. So that's why this guide is in your hands. It's here to make you the best you can be who will succeed on your climb up the ladder of achievement and follow your dreams.

This book is your how-to guide on how to become a flawless writer, filled with exercises, explanations, and examples. The best way to become a better writer is to practice, practice, and practice. Within this guide, you will have the opportunity to complete exercises that will make you a pro at using correct grammar. Repetition *always* helps you succeed. By the time you complete this book, you will write succinct, straightforward essays that will almost guarantee admission into the college of your dreams.

In this book, you will:

- Learn grammar mechanics, such as comma slices, run-on sentences, and correct word choices

- Read several examples that will show you how to write great sentences

- Practice exercises on your own for grammar mechanics, sentence structure, and the writing process

- Go through the writing process, such as brainstorming, outlining your essay, and writing a well-written paper

- Understand different writing styles and essays, such as personal essays, expository essays, argumentative essays, query letters, research papers, blog posts, emails, and narrative essays.

- Be able to write an effective essay with strong diction, tight focus, and expressive meaning

Don't feel overwhelmed by the amount of terms, rules, and work you will be doing in this guide. Remember that it's here to help you, not bog you down. This isn't your average guide either; instead of rushing through each chapter and trying to finish it all within a short amount of time, work at your own pace. The slower you go, the more this guide will be beneficial to you, guaranteed.

Now, onto some grammar rules—Happy Writing!

PART 1
Grammar Basics

This portion of the guide reviews all major concepts of grammar. You may think, *this is why I slept through every single English class*, but it's time to crack down and truly learn correct grammar. Each chapter provides explanations, examples, and exercises. Work through each chapter slowly, and make sure you understand why answers are correct for each exercise.

This section includes the foundations of grammar, such as nouns, pronouns, adjectives, adverbs, verbs, and other elements. Part 1 also goes over parts of a sentence, such as prepositional phrases, spelling guidelines, and capitalization rules. Although this section is the hardest and most arduous to plough through, all the toil will be worth it in the end. The road to flawless writing is a difficult journey made by few, but it's not impossible to complete it.

Once you've mastered this grammar section, you will move onto writing mechanics and improve your sentences. Afterward, you will move to the writing process.

"The greater part of the world's troubles
are due to questions of grammar."

- MICHEL DE MONTAIGNE

CHAPTER 1

What is Grammar and Why is it Important?

Tackling grammar isn't an easy task. Building good grammar skills begins at an early age, so trying to relearn every single grammar rule is hard to do. However, you *can* do it. But first, let's break down what grammar is, what it consists of, and why it's important in regards to sentence structure and overall writing style.

According to a 2013 study from PR Daily, 11 percent of students across the country feel that electronic communications had a negative impact on their writing skills, yet 86 percent of teens think having good writing skills is important for success in life. So why do teens struggle with good grammar skills so much? The answer is technology and other types of electronic communication. Because teens shorten a vast majority of words, they open themselves up to more spelling errors, incorrect grammar usage, and fragmented sentences that lack focus, clarity and brevity. But bad grammar and writing skills affect teens' grades and admission into college, setting them up for failure. However, you don't need to be another statistic; you can change that with practice and hard work.

As defined in the dictionary, grammar is "the whole system and structure of a language or of languages in general". Essentially, grammar mechanics are the connecting pieces of good sentence structure. In order to write great sentences, you must master grammar. It's usually the most mundane part of the job, but also the most important. But let's further discover why grammar is so important to motivate you further.

There are three ways that grammar improves your life:

- **Makes you stand out:** If you're a teen who writes eloquently and will little to no grammar errors, then you're a rarity! When applying for internships, racing for the valedictorian spot, or wanting to get into your dream college, your personal essay sometimes determines whether you will earn that spot or not. Your writing style speaks so much about you to others, so don't you want to stand out from the crowd?

- **Prepares you for the future:** Yes, you're only in high school now, but one day you want to fulfill your dream of becoming a doctor, teacher, engineer, or writer. So how will you get there? Through hard work and amazing writing skills, and creating those skills takes time and practice. If you start reading good material every day (from online news articles to novels) and voraciously write daily, then you'll become a great writer without even realizing it.

- **Helps you communicate well in general:** Apart from your future career, grammar helps you communicate well. Want to ask out that cute girl in your science class? You need great grammar skills for that. Need to ask your boss for a day off to get a few things done? It will take a few persuasive words to convince him to grant your wish. Communication is key to function well in society and in relationships.

There are countless other reasons why correct grammar is vital to write well, but theses reasons are the most important. But enough about repeating why grammar is so important—let's begin your review.

Most Common Grammar Mistakes

Even though high school students (and adults) struggle with different grammar and writing errors, there are some common mistakes that almost everyone battles with, such as *your* and *you're*; *there*, *their*, and *they're*; *its* and *it's*; *whom* and *who*; pronoun errors; and run-on sentences (comma splices). These blaring errors, if made on an important article or document, look really bad and will sometimes cost you a good letter grade or job. So let's review these top common grammar mistakes.

Your and You're

This, perhaps, is the most common grammar mistake (and the most easily fixable). If you use either of these in the wrong context, then this will hurt your writing reputation. For instance, if you're writing a personal essay for college admission, then using correct spelling speaks highly of you as a student and shows that you will succeed in that university. There is a quick and easy way to make sure that you use both correctly:

First off, *your* is a possessive form. It determines that something belongs to you (i.e. your car, your father, or your life).

Some **examples** include:

> James, come pick up **your** clothes. They are all over the floor.
>
> While you were out, **your** pet frog decided to do a couple of cool tricks.
>
> Can you please tell us **your** home address?

On the other hand, *you're* is a shortened contraction of *you are*. So many students interchange these words even though they have entirely different meanings.

Some examples of *you're* include:

> Whether **you're** going to the movies or not, I need to start getting ready.
>
> I've have met a ton of sarcastic people in my life, but **you're** the wittiest person ever.
>
> **You're** going to love the new football field that's opening in a few weeks.

A quick tip that will always determine the correct meaning is by asking yourself if "you are" would fit into the sentence. For instance, would "you are" fit nicely into this sentence: *With practice, your confidence will improve with peers.* If you had used you're, then the sentence would not make sense (i.e. *You are* confidence will improve…). Once you take the time to think about how your or you're is used in the sentence, then you will always get it correct, guaranteed.

Use these exercises below to help improve your grammar skills, in regards to *your* and *you're*. Circle the correct answer. All answers are included in the back of the book.

EXERCISE A: Your and You're

A.1 Curtis, why did you decide to take _____ dog to the park instead of study for chemistry? (your, you're)

A.2 If you know that _____ invited to the party, then why are you not going? (your, you're)

A.3 Just because _____ not popular doesn't mean that nobody likes you. (your, you're)

A.4 I don't care what you say; _____ in love with Ryan Gosling just like every other girl. (your, you're)

A.5 I can't believe how incredible _____ movie collection is! (your, you're)

There, Their, and They're

Using these three words correctly in a sentence is also one of the most common errors made by students. If you slow down and take the time to figure out which word correctly fits in the sentence, then you'll always get it right. Most mistakes are made because students rush through writing sentences and don't double-check their correct word usage. Below are quick definitions for each word. Knowing the definitions will help you remember which words to use in different scenarios.

There represents a place and has **two** main uses: it can either mean an unspecified place or can be used to show that something exists. Some examples include:

> Look at that lovely flower over **there**!
>
> **There** used to be so many trees in the park, but they were cut down.
>
> I wonder if **there** will be enough food left at the party for us.

Their is used to show possession, just like *your*, *his*, *her*, *its*, *our*, and *my*. As a little trick to remember when to use *their*, substitute *our* instead of *their*. If it makes sense in the sentence, then using *their* is correct. Read some examples below:

> **Their** dog knows how to play dead so well!
>
> Lydia, have you seen **their** new car?
>
> I told you that **their** house is for sale, Paul!

They're is the shortened version of *they are*. The best way to tell when to use *they're* is to insert *they are* into the sentence to see whether it makes sense or not. Some examples include:

They're here to take the test for the university's admissions.

Do you know whether **they're** ready to move in together?

Until Annabelle finishes high school, **they're** not going to leave Holly Heights.

To get better at choosing the right word to use, below are a few exercises to practice with:

EXERCISE B: There, Their, and They're

B.1 Have you noticed that _____ pets are not well behaved at all? (they're, their, there)

B.2 Kyle, _____ here! (they're, their, there)

B.3 Can you please put the chairs over _____, please? (they're, their, there)

B.4 Isabelle, _____ are the supplies that we were looking for! (they're, their, there)

B.5 Do you know _____ children very well? (they're, their, there)

B.6 _____ the reason why we are here. (they're, their, there)

As stated before, knowing the difference between *their, they're,* and *there* is very simple if you take the time to use each word correctly. Using these words incorrectly on a job application, essay, or even on social media could be detrimental. Your use of bad grammar will show potential employers, teachers, or other adults that may not deserve a job or get accepted into that particular university.

Pronoun-Antecedent Errors

Pronoun-antecedent errors are some of the most common grammatical errors made, too. In natural conversation, people use pronouns incorrectly all the time—and without even realizing it. But when you use pronouns in any type or written format (whether it's an email or essay), you need to use them correctly.

Here are some examples of commonly misused pronoun antecedent:

Incorrect: The family are going on a picnic tomorrow.

Correct: The family is going on a picnic tomorrow.

Remember that group nouns are considered singular, so they need a singular pronoun. Some common pronoun-antecedent errors include: herd, family, group, somebody, anyone, everyone, anyone, etc.

> **Tip:** A **pronoun** is a word that is substituted for a noun. An **antecedent** is a word for which a pronoun stands. (The pronoun must agree with its antecedent in number, too.)

The following examples are pairs of pronouns and antecedents:

- **President George Washington** fought with **his** fellow soldiers with honor and glory.
- The **stack** of papers sits on **its** shelf.
- **Everyone** fends for **himself** or **herself** in this classroom.
- **Each** of the teachers **has** to do a presentation for the headmaster.
- **Some** of the apples fell out of **their** bag.

- **Jane** and **Haley** combined **their** birthday parties and threw one huge party.

- **Neither** the dog **nor** the trainer knew what their routine was.

There are a several of ways to come across pronoun-antecedent agreements, so you will mentally have to be aware when the pronoun and antecedent are plural or singular, such as *somebody is here* and *some are coming to the fair.*

Some examples include:

EXERCISE C: Pronoun-Antecedent Errors

C.1   Either Jim or Hannah _____ available to help out at the garage sale. (is, are)

C.2   The can of apple juice dripped _____ contents all over the floor. (its, their)

C.3   _____ anybody confused about the chemistry assignment? (is, are)

C.4   Some of the glitter fell out of _____ container (its, their).

Run-on Sentences (Or Comma Splices)

Run-on sentences, also known as comma splices, are compound sentences that aren't punctuated correctly. Most students struggle with correct punctuation (which will be discussed later in this book), so run-on sentences are very common. There are some rules to remember when avoiding making run-on sentences:

- When joining two compound sentences, use a coordinating conjunction (and put a comma in front of it). Coordinating conjunctions include *and*, *but*, *nor*, *or*, *yet*, *for*, and *so*.

  Fiona loves eating nectarines**, but** George loves eating bananas.

- When you don't use a coordinating conjunction, link the sentences by using a semicolon (;).

  Harry Potter loved his friends**;** he'd do anything to keep them safe.

The following are some exercises for you to practice with. Determine which sentences are either correct or incorrect:

EXERCISE D: Run-on Sentences (Or Comma Splices)

D.1 I don't know if I completed my college application; there was a huge list of requirements to fulfill. (correct or incorrect)

D.2 It's up to Sarah to decide whether I should go I don't think I was invited to the party. (correct or incorrect)

D.3 Mrs. Tanner graded our English papers unfairly my paper took an entire week to write. (correct or incorrect)

D.4 Yvonne didn't know that the history test was on Monday because she missed all last week of school. (correct or incorrect)

Correct punctuation is the key to avoiding run-on sentences. The grammar mistake is easily fixed with the correct use of a coordinating conjunction or a semicolon. Punctuation will be discussed more in depth in Chapter 12 in Part 2.

It's and Its

Using *it's* and *its* correctly easily confuses most students, yet it's an easy fix. If you take the time to determine which word makes sense in the sentence, then you will always end up using the correct word.

It's is the contraction of *it is*, which is also a combination of a singular subject and verb.

It's that time of year again to bring out your winter clothes.

Whether **it's** Mexican or Chinese cuisine, I can eat it every night.

Can you believe that **it's** going to rain all weekend?

Its is a possessive form of a singular subject.

> The moose was very protective of **its** newborn.
>
> The dog licked **its** paw after eating a delicious meal.
>
> I can't tell where **its** mother came from.

Sometimes, writers use the word *its'* but that's not a word at all; don't let it fool you! That isn't a word at all, so don't let yourself think that it is one.

Below are exercises to determine which word is used correctly in each sentence. Circle the answer.

EXERCISE E: It's and Its

E.1 Can we see its home, please? This animal looks malnourished. (correct or incorrect)

E.2 Whether its convenient or not, please take your young brother home. (correct or incorrect)

E.3 It's the happiest time of year when all the Christmas decorations are up and everyone is cheery. (correct or incorrect)

E.4 Do you know if it's time to go? I don't want to be late for its checkup. (correct or incorrect)

E.5 Dr. Henry said its not looking too well for our sports teams this year. (correct, incorrect)

Whom vs. Who

Students incorrectly substituted *who* and *whom* all the time because both words sound correct in the wrong sentence. However, there are a few tricks that will help you remember when to use either *who* or *whom*.

Who is a subjective pronoun and is most commonly used in sentences. (A **subjective pronoun** is the subject of a verb.)

> **Who** is that over there?
>
> It was Emily Dickinson **who** wrote beautiful poetry from her bedroom.
>
> Bonnie, **who** won the first-place prize, stood on the podium looking proud.

Whom is in the objective case. (An **objective pronoun** is a pronoun that is the object of a verb.) Whom isn't used as much, but still appears in sentences from time to time. Even well-educated scholars get who and whom confused very often. However, if you understand the purpose of both words, then you will use them correctly from now on.

> To **whom** were you referring?
>
> Krista, **whom** the test was given to, didn't score very well.
>
> Can you give this shirt to **whom** it belongs?

In order to remember when to either use who or whom, ask yourself whether he or him could substitute for who and whom. So if the sentence sounds good with he, then who is the right word to use. If the sentence sounds better with him, then the correct word is whom.

Below are some exercises for you to practice with. Determine whether *who* or *whom* should be in the sentence.

EXERCISE F: Whom vs. Who

F.1 Do you know _____ this belongs to? (who, whom)

F.2 Heisenberg? _____ is he? (who, whom)

F.3 Plato, _____ wrote *The Republic*, is one of the most celebrated Greek philosophers of all time. (who, whom)

F.4 _____ can we depend on to finish our project in a few hours? (who, whom)

Conclusion

Tackling habitual grammar mistakes and mastering correct grammar mechanics is tough. Most adults, let alone high school students, don't try to improve their grammar at all, so give yourself a break if you still make mistakes. Over time, your grammar will improve. In the mean time, keep working at it, and reward yourself when you learn something new.

Using perfect grammar can't happen overnight, necessarily. But with continued practice, reading daily, and studying great writing from the greats. You don't have to love Victorian literature to become a great writer. Reading articles online will improve your writing just as well. All that you need is diligence, practice, and a reading schedule.

Hopefully this chapter helped you eliminate a few repetitive grammar mistakes for you—and it's only the beginning. The rest of Part 1 is filled with other common grammatical mistakes and quick overviews of the essential elements of a sentence. You survived your first chapter, so let's jump into the next one, shall we?

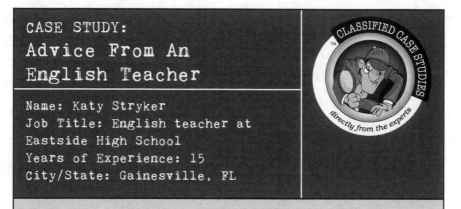

CASE STUDY:
Advice From An English Teacher

Name: Katy Stryker
Job Title: English teacher at Eastside High School
Years of Experience: 15
City/State: Gainesville, FL

Q What are some of the most common grammar and writing mistakes you've seen?

The most common grammatical errors are some that I also see in college-educated fellow teachers: in agreement (such as subject-verb: i.e. "they is" & pronoun-antecedent: "everyone had their..."). Other common errors include mixing up homophones (close/clothes; know/no, etc.), which can often be caught and corrected if people would simply reread things before turning them in. A lot is and always has been two words!

Q How do you try to improve/teach students how to use better grammar and writing styles?

I try to emphasize the importance of knowing the rules, whether we use them everyday or not—so that when you're writing that college essay or in that interview, you know what to say. (I also recommend they practice using their best conventions and rereading/correcting before turning things in, even on everyday work, so they make the correct habits and don't accidentally make errors.

In my "College Prep" class, we also use grammar pre- and post-tests to see growth. Then, in almost daily mini-lessons, we focus on the most common errors. I've found the older the students are, the harder it is to change habits. Since English is such a complicated language with many exceptions, the "caught ya's" we used previously have been found to be too overwhelming for most; instead practicing the correct structure repeatedly (or Jeff Anderson's Mechanically Inclined books), such as commas in a series, provide correct use and good habit making.

Q What do you recommend for students to do in order to improve on their own?

There are many free online programs (such as NoRedInk) which provide individuated remediation and which self check, so the feedback is immediate and personalized. Also, after we complete a process paper (more than just an in-class write), which should have been edited before turning in, I have each student note and record the specific errors he or she is making.

Q Why is it important for students (especially in high school) to have good grammar and writing skills?

The written word is the way we communicate our ideas; if we want to prove our intelligence, mastery of a subject, or even simply share our viewpoints, not only does the diction matter, but the polished product is a reflection of how valid and valuable those words are. Although, with 24/7 Internet access, the world is seemingly getting smaller, however, the competition is getting greater. It seems wise to present yourself as strongly as possible.

Q Any additional advice for students?

The more types of writing you read and then think about which writing is most effective, and the more you write consciously and deliberately, the better a writer you will become!

CHAPTER 2
Spelling and Capitalization

Spelling, especially in the English language, is very difficult to learn. There are so many rules and exceptions that it's hard to keep track of every single one. Most new English speakers struggle with spelling the most because it's so difficult to remember each exception. However, there are a few easy rules that will help you remember how to spell correctly. This section is a brief overview of common misspellings and rules to follow. Exercises are included at the end of each rule, and wealth of examples are given. Answers to each exercise are provided in the back of this guide, too.

For a quick overview, some of the most common misspellings that will be discussed include *accept* and *except*; *affect* and *effect*; *we're*, *where*, and *were*; *to*, *two*, and *too*; *advise* and *advice*, *then* and *than*; *led* and *lead*; *conscious* and *conscience*.

The rest of the section will go through the "I before E" rule and some spelling exceptions. Correct spelling comes with much reading and practice. Don't rush through this section if you don't have a good handle on spelling. Take your time to refresh yourself with the rules and complete the exercises to become a spelling master.

Most Common Misspellings

Accept and Except

Accept is a verb that means to consent and receive, such as:

> Daniel **accepted** the free extra credit.
>
> Please **accept** this as a token of friendship.
>
> I **accepted** the job offer!

Except is a preposition that means to not include or other than, such as:

> I go to dance class every day **except** Tuesdays.
>
> **Except** Julie, everyone wanted to watch the new horror flick.

These words are totally different parts of speech, so misusing them will throw off the entire meaning of your sentence. The following are exercises for you to practice with:

EXERCISE A: Accept and Except

A.1   Billy, will you _____ my apology? (accept, except)

A.2   Why can't you _____ the fact that I'm going to clown school? (accept, except)

A.3   _____ this weekend, I'm available to go out of town in the future. (accept, except)

A.4   _____ this piece of advice and move on from the situation. (accept, except)

A.5   Sydney can go _____ for the fact that she broke her leg last week. (accept, except)

Affect and Effect

Affect is a verb that means to have an influence on, such as:

> Hurricane Katrina **affected** the lives of thousands of people who lived in New Orleans.
> Whether or not this will **affect** you doesn't matter at the moment.

Effect is a noun that means a change that is the result or consequence of an action or other cause, such as:

> The **effect** of the atomic bomb still impacts Hiroshima and other parts of Japan.
> Why does caffeine have such a crazy **effect** on you?

Or, can be a verb that means to bring about, such as

> The Obamacare policy has **effected** change in the entire healthcare system in America.

Both of these words are very similar in meaning, but are different parts of speech. As a little trick to help you remember when to use affect or effect, think about the acronym **RAVEN**: **R**emember, **A**ffect is a **V**erb and **E**ffect is a **N**oun (The OWL at Purdue, 2014).

Below are exercises to help you practice:

EXERCISE B: Affect and Effect

B.1 The exhilarating _____ that this espresso shot is having over me is too much! (affect, effect)

B.2 While this may not _____ you now, it'll hurt you sometime in the future. (affect, effect)

B.3 Style icon Vera Wang's fall outfit choices will _____ women and how they dress this season. (affect, effect)

B.4 I thought this _____ would produce good change. (affect, effect)

If you're still struggling with *affect* and *effect*, check out Purdue's Online Writing Lab for more helpful tips.

We're, Were, and Where

These three words are commonly interchanged in sentences, but have vastly different meanings. If you use them incorrectly, then this will look bad in front of employees, teachers, peers, and other adults. Using *we're*, *where*, and *were* correctly is easy if you take the time to remember their meanings.

We're is the contraction form of "we are".

> **We're** going to the first opening night of the annual corn maze!
>
> I think **we're** late, Ben.

Were is a linking verb that means to have a quality of being.

> They **were** just telling me how funny your laugh is.
>
> As of a half an hour ago, there **were** 10 cupcakes here.

Where either refers to a place or asks a question.

> **Where** are you taking me?
>
> Do you know **where** your socks are?
>
> This is the place **where** we first met.

Below are some practice exercises. Fill in the blanks with the correct word.

EXERCISE C: We're, Were, and Where

C.1 Do you know _____ dinner is at on Wednesday? (we're, were, where)

C.2 Remember, _____ in this together. (we're, were, where)

C.3 I distinctly recall that there _____ two pies here, but now they're gone. (we're, were, where)

C.4 _____ you planning on coming to the lake on Saturday? (we're, were, where)

C.5 _____ do you think our next vacation will be? (we're, were, where)

C.6 Did you know that _____ hosting the next dinner party this month? (we're, were, where)

To, Two, and Too

The words **to**, **two**, and **too** get easily confused as well. As previously stated, if you pay attention to their meanings, then you'll always use them correctly.

To can be used as a preposition before a noun or as an infinitive before a verb.

Please take me **to** the store.

Do you need **to** start singing right now?

Two is the written word for the number "2".

The **two** sisters skipped down the street.

At age **two**, Juliet knew how to play a scale on the piano.

Too is a synonym for also or can indicate overindulgence before a verb.

I think this pizza has **too** much cheese.

Wow, I love the Smiths, **too**!

Below are exercises to practice when to use *to*, *two*, and *too*. Fill in the blanks with the correct word.

EXERCISE D: To, Two, and Too

D.1   There are _____ reasons why I own a cat. (to, two, too)

D.2   Besides football, I really love basketball,_____. (to, two, too)

D.3   Gina loves _____ help out during Saturdays. (to, two, too)

D.4   Remember _____ take out the trash tonight. (to, two, too)

D.5   I_____ play the guitar from time to time. (to, two, too)

D.6   The _____ most famous novels by Jane Austen are *Pride and Prejudice* and *Emma*. (to, two, too)

Advice and Advise

Interchanging *advice* and *advise* is very easy to do, but they have different meanings (once again). Make sure you understand what they mean so you use them correctly in sentences.

Advice is a noun that means to give an opinion or suggestion.

> Daisy, your grandma's **advice** is good, and you should listen to it.
>
> The best **advice** I can give you is to remain calm.

Advise is a verb form of giving an opinion or suggestion.

> I **advise** you to starting studying now for your final exam.
>
> Mr. Herman **advised** me to take British Literature in the spring.

The following exercises will help you practice when to use *advice* and *advise* correctly. Fill in the blanks.

EXERCISE E: Advice and Advise

E.1 Can you give me some good _____? (advice, advise)

E.2 Jodi, will you _____ me how to finish this project? (advice, advise)

E.3 Mrs. Kim will _____ you how make the best apple pie. (advice, advise)

E.4 Thank you for the _____, Holly! (advice, advise)

Then and Than

Confusing ***then*** and ***than*** happens very often, especially in formal, written communication. Using these words correctly is vital when you're writing an essay or applying for a job. Make sure you understand their correct meanings.

Then is an adverb that usually relates to time or connects a sentence.

> What time is dinner **then**?
>
> If the Red Sox keep winning, **then** they will go to the play-offs.

Than is a word that insinuates a comparison.

> Rather **than** going to the movies, let's go stargazing.
>
> Other **than** working at the coffee shop, I help out at the pizza restaurants on Tuesdays and Thursdays.

Below are exercises to help practice. Fill in the blanks with the correct word.

EXERCISE F: Then and Than

F.1 I chose to go to class rather _____ skip. (then, than)

F.2 If I can't go, _____ you can't go. (then, than)

F.3 Do you know where we are meeting _____? (then, than)

F.4 Would you rather take calculus _____ AP statistics? (then, than)

Led and Lead

Once again, most students use *led* and *lead* wrong. Study their meanings and make sure you use them correctly.

Led is the past tense verb of showing somebody the way to somewhere.

> He **led** me down this beautiful trail on Sunday.
>
> George Washington bravely **led** his fellow soldiers during battle.

Lead usually means a toxic metallic element.

> Have you heard about the **lead** poisoning scandal recently?
>
> The **lead** pencil broke during her stressful exam.

The following exercises will help you practice using *led* and *lead* correctly. Fill in the blanks.

EXERCISE G: Led and Lead

G.1 The preschool teacher _____ her students from the playground to their classroom. (led, lead)

G.2 I'm not sure if this _____ pencil is okay to use. (led, lead)

G.3 Is there _____ paint on this car? (led, lead)

G.4 Yvonne _____ her toddler along the sidewalk. (led, lead).

Conscious and Conscience

Even though these words have different meanings, they sound and are spelled similarly. Make sure you understand their meanings, and commit them to memory.

Conscious means being aware of yourself or the world around you.

> Ever since I spilled cheese on my sweater, I feel **conscious** now.
>
> I walk **consciously** now when I get home super late so I don't disturb my family.

Conscience is a moral understanding or an inner feeling.

> Do you have a **conscience** or not?
>
> My **conscience** is telling me that we shouldn't do this.

Below are some exercises to practice with. Fill in the blanks, or circle the correct word.

EXERCISE H: Conscious and Conscience

H.1 We need to make a _____ decision soon. (conscious, conscience)

H.2 What is your _____ telling you? (conscious, conscience)

H.3 I wish people were more _____ about recycling and saving the earth. (conscious, conscience)

H.4 I just don't feel like he has a _____ (conscious, conscience)

The "I Before E" Rule

Knowing and memorizing the "I Before E" rule is very efficient and will help you spell correctly in the future. The witty spelling tool goes "I before E except after C, or when sounding like A, as in neighbor and weigh". Remember this rhyme, and you'll always spell tricky words correctly. Some examples include:

"I Before E…": Die, lie, fiend, and quiet

"….Except after C…": receive, deceive, and achieve

"…Or when sounding like A": rein, neighbor, and weigh

When you suddenly stumble over how to spell certain words correctly, say this catchy rhyme to yourself and you're bound to spell the word right.

Vowels and Silent E's

Vowels trick writers up all the time, so this section will quickly go over them. In general, vowels include *a, e, o,* and *i*. All other letters are considered consonants. Because vowels can make similar sounds, it's easy to misplace them in words.

Here are some examples below:

Incorrect: I ate the last avacado.
Correct: I ate the last avocado.

Incorrect: Can you pass the balsamic vinagrette across the table to me?
Correct: Can you pass the balsamic vinaigrette across the table to me?

Even though a vowel may sound correct in a word, it isn't always the correct vowel to use. With much practice and memorization, you'll be able to use the right vowels in words.

Plural Form and Endings

Using the correct plural from (also now as endings) can get quite tricky, too. The English language has so many exceptions, so using the correct plural ending is sometimes not as easy as it seems.

Here are the most common plural endings:

s

es

i

Besides these endings, some words stay the same and don't have an additional ending. Here are some examples below:

Singular: cat
Plural: cats

Singular: bus
Plural: busses

Singular: syllabus
Plural: syllabi

Before writing plural endings, it's important to ask yourself if the plural ending is correct or not. Through practice and reading, you'll be able to use the correct plural endings every time.

Suffixes and Prefixes

Although you probably don't misspell suffixes and prefixes that often, it's good to do a review of what they are and what they mean.

Prefixes are a word or letter placed in front of another word. *Suffixes* are a word or letter that comes at the end of another word. You see prefixes and suffixes all the time, but probably aren't aware of them. Let's look at some examples to help you get a better understanding of it.

Here are the most common prefixes and suffixes:

ROOTS	MEANING	EXAMPLES
A, ac, ad, af, ag, al, an, ap, as, at	To, toward, near, in addition to, by	Aside, annihilate, aggression, attempt, assuage
Ab, abs	Off, away	Abrupt, Absolve, Abdicate
-acy, -cy	State or quality	Privacy, advocacy
Dis, dif	Separate, reverse	Disregard, differ
-en	To become	Straighten, strengthen
-ing	Acting	Swimming, climbing

After examining these examples, you've probably noticed that you speak and write tons of words that have prefixes and suffixes in them. If you study prefixes and suffixes and their root meanings, then your writing will improve by great strides. They are the key to helping you become an impeccable speller.

Exceptions to the Spelling Rules

The English language is full of random exceptions. Memorizing them would be too difficult and, quite frankly, there would be no point. However, be aware that they exist; you may spell some correctly already without being aware of it. Unfortunately, you can't make your mind remember each exception, but there are other ways that you can remember them without sitting down and studying them. The best activity to do is to read, read, read. Read anything that you want, too. The more you read, the more you'll become to be natural speller.

Capitalization

Capitalization is writing a letter uppercased, followed by lowercase letters. In other countries, such as Germany, most nouns are capitalized, but not so in English. Although most nouns are lowercased, it stills helpful to remember rules for capitalization. Let's work through them below.

Rule #1: Always capitalize names.

This rule may seem obvious, but it's a good one to become familiar with again. Let's look at some examples below.

> Jenna took me to soccer practice on Thursday.
>
> Although they were running late, Pamela and Gwen took the train to Paris.
>
> At the end of the day, Tim is my best friend who has my back.

There is never an exception to capitalizing names, so this rule is good to remember. Let's move onto the next rule, shall we?

Rule #2: Always capitalize proper nouns

Remembering to capitalize proper nouns is quite easy, but detecting what a proper noun is can get quite tricky. Most proper nouns that need to be capitalized include names of cities, states, streets, and names of events and famous places. Here are some examples below.

In Berlin, we toured the famous landmarks and buildings.

If you turn a left on Main Street, you'll find the Chinese restaurant pretty easily.

Under the cabinet hid Tessa the cat.

Remember to capitalize proper nouns in sentences, no matter what position they're at in a sentence. After practice you'll become a master at it. Now let's move on to the last rule.

Rule #3: Always capitalize the first letter in a sentence.

This rule is quite easy and simple, but it's still good to go over. You might not capitalize the first letter in a sentence when texting friends, but when writing academic papers or even in just everyday writing, you should always capitalize the first letter in a sentence. Let's view a few examples below.

Just like Anna, Silas is going to Gabriel's 10th birthday party.

Would you like to accompany me to the cafeteria?

The trees were swaying in the ocean breeze.

After going through these rules, let's practice using good capitalization skills on the following page.

Below are exercises that ask you to capitalize the correct words in the sentence. Answers are provided in the back of the book.

EXERCISE I: Capitalization

I.1 on the 8th day, our dog penny found her way back home after being lost!

I.2 When will sesame street be on TV again?

I.3 Beneath the bridge were two cats named patty and maddy.

I.4 Although denise lives on hampton avenue, I still visit her a lot.

I.5 other than that, Kevin is a pretty awesome kid.

I.6 tommy didn't enjoy his birthday for some reason.

I.7 Can you take me to mount rushmore one day soon?

I.8 Please take matilda to the nurse's office.

I.9 did you see who climbed mount everest the other day?

I.10 Where can I take my little sister jamie to play outside?

Conclusion

Keep in mind that spelling isn't an easy mistake to fix, nor is capitalization. Breaking wrong habits takes diligence and practice, but it can be done. Without correct spelling and capitalization, your sentence won't make sense and will be considered useless. Making sure this basic building block is corrected is vital, so become a spelling master as quickly as possible.

You may feel overwhelmed by reading through all of these rules, examples, and exercises, but don't fret. If you need to reread certain sections, take your time and do so. Once you get into a routine of reading magazines, news sources, or books and practice exercises, then spelling and capitalizing words correctly will be very easy for you. In the back of the guide are additional links if you are seeking additional help.

CHAPTER 3:
Adjectives and Adverbs

Some other parts of speech include adjectives and adverbs. These can be considered the "flavors" of a sentence and add description to an otherwise brief sentence. A few great writers believe that adverbs weaken sentences, so therefore they should not be used. However, there are instances when adverbs make sentence alive. Either way, it's important to understand the technical definition of adjectives and adverbs, so this chapter reviews both elements.

As you go through this chapter, look over each definition, example, and exercise for a brief review. Most students struggle with interchanging adjectives and adverbs and using them incorrectly, which considerably weaken their writing. Don't let this happen to you; it's a very correctable mistake if you pay attention to their definitions. Memorize these definitions and rules so your writing will improve and you won't make the same mistake as them. Your writing will become immensely better after going through this chapter thoroughly.

An *adjective* is a word or string of words that modify a noun or pronoun. They sometimes may appear before the word they modify. Adjectives also answer the questions *which*, *what kind*, *and how many*? Some examples include:

The bathroom is so **pretty** now after its makeover.

Penelope, do you own the **red** or **blue** backpack?

Adjectives also come in three degrees, such as **positive, comparative,** and **superlative** degrees, and are used for comparison.

POSITIVE	COMPARATIVE	SUPERLATIVE
Bad	Worse	Worst
Quick	Quicker	Quickest
Affluent	More Affluent	Most Affluent

One rule to remember is that *good* is an adjective but is sometimes mistaken for an adverb. Although *well* is usually an adverb, it can be used as an adjective, such as when referring to health. Below are examples:

Correct: Today is a **good** day.

Incorrect: I'm feeling **good**, thank you for asking.

Correct: I'm feeling **well** today.

Below are exercises to practice using adjectives. Fill in the blanks with your own adjectives. Suggestions are provided in the back of the book.

EXERCISE A: Adjectives

A.1   Vivian bought new _____ shoes for a great price.

A.2   Why on earth would you buy that _____ outfit?

A.3   My _____ project isn't going as well as I had planned.

A.4   David began composing his _____ manifesto.

A.5   The football team had a _____ season.

An *adverb* is a word or set of words that modifies verbs, other adverbs, or adjectives. They also answer the questions *how, when, where, and how much?*

> Think **quickly**, please!
>
> I really don't believe that he thinks that **badly** of you.

Some rules relating to adverbs include:

1. Usually, adverbs end in *–ly*, but others don't. In general, if *–ly* can be added to the adjective form, place it there to form an adverb.

    > The doctor **adamantly** said to exercise more often.
    >
    > He was hired **solely** based off of his great writing skills.

2. Adverbs that answer the question *how* sometimes cause grammatical problems. Determining if *–ly* should be attached can be difficult. Adverbs are often misplaced in sentences, which require adjectives instead.

    > The principal peered **angrily** over her glasses.
    >
    > She pranced so **annoyingly** over toward us that I decided to leave.

Below are some exercises to practice using adverbs correctly. Fill in the blanks with the proper adverb.

EXERCISE B: Adverbs

B.1   I think I know how to crack proofs _____ well. (fair, fairly)

B.2   Can you speak more _____? (clear, clearly)

B.3   She _____ took haphazard parts and invented a cool creation. (clever, cleverly)

B.4   I _____ doubt that the band won't come out for an encore. (high, highly)

B.5   Do you come here _____? (regular, regularly)

Tip: Having a Handbook Handy

Why You Should Buy One:

Although it's the last thing you want to read, owning and using a grammar handbook will boost your writing very quickly and efficiently. Grammar handbooks are a condensed version of grammar rules, writing tips, and other rules about writing. Their main purpose is to have quick and easy access to looking up different rules about grammar.

What Types of Handbooks You Should Buy:

Below is a list of great handbooks that will improve not only your grammar skills but also your writing in general.

- *The Elements of Style* by William Strunk Jr.
- *On Writing: A Memoir of the Craft* by Stephen King
- *Eats, Shoots & Leaves: The Zero Tolerance Approach to Punctuation* by Lynne Truss

There are a plethora of other handbooks, but these are some of the best-selling handbooks and are quite effective.

Where to Purchase One:

You can purchase a handbook online or in any bookstore. If you have trouble locating one, you can ask an employee for advice.

Conclusion

Understanding adjectives and adverbs is fairly simple. After viewing their definitions, it's easy to see that adjectives and adverbs are very different from each other. As a general rule, it's better to use adjectives in sentences rather than adverbs. (And sometimes, adjectives can replace adverbs altogether.) However, you can still include adverbs in sentences as long as they don't overwhelm the meaning of the sentence. Sometimes, fewer words in a sentence make it that much stronger and better.

Hopefully this section was useful and helped you get a good grasp of adjectives, adverbs, and their rules. Don't beat yourself up if you still use them incorrectly sometimes. It just means that you need to go back and review the material better. Every student struggles with different rules and concepts, so don't feel embarrassed if you don't fully grasp adjectives and adverbs. If you need to, review the rules and definitions again. In the back of the book are additional links and online exercises.

"This is just the sort of nonsense up with which I will not put."

- WINSTON S. CHURCHILL

CHAPTER 4
Articles and Appositives

You may have read the title of this chapter and thought, *Um, what are articles and appositives? I never learned this...*

Most likely, you have learned this stuff. Don't let the technical terminology frighten you. Believe it or not, you probably use articles and appositives in daily conversation.

Some high school students struggle with knowing how to use articles and appositives correctly, let alone understand their definitions. This section is a brief review of articles of appositives and includes examples and exercises. The words "articles" and "appositives" shouldn't stress you out because more than likely you already know how to use them. Knowing their technical terms and reviewing where they are in a sentence will help you write better.

Take your time to understand each definition and study each example. Articles and appositives are tricky parts of speech that are sometimes not taught in elementary school. However, after reviewing their definitions, you will discover that you happen to use them in everyday life (you just didn't know it!). Feel free to go through this section as slowly or quickly as you desire. You as the student know when you understand a concept.

So let's dive into understanding articles and appositives.

An **article** is a type of adjective, which is always used with a noun and provides information about it. The two articles are **a/an** and **the**. They help clarify their object better in a sentence. Some examples include:

A/an is an indefinite article because the noun it is paired with is indefinite or general. These articles don't give detailed descriptions about their objects.

> Zara is **an** anteater that was recently brought to the zoo.
>
> **A** little boy smiled when he saw that his daddy was home.

Below are exercises that will help you practice when to use **a** or **an**. Fill in the blanks, or circle the correct word.

EXERCISE A: A or An

A.1 Excuse me, did you happen to find _____ iguana around here? (a, an)

A.2 Yes, the food fight in the cafeteria started with _____ thrown Hershey's bar. (a, an)

A.3 Can you believe that Diana is _____ track star? (a, an)

A.4 High up in the sky, _____ airplane passed over us. (a, an)

The is a definite article and indicates a specific thing. Some examples include:

> This is **the** book I want to read at the moment.
>
> Are you sure that this is **the** dog that you want?

Below are some exercises that will make you either pick *a/an* or ***the***. Fill in the blanks, or circle the correct word.

EXERCISE B: Articles

B.1 Maggie is _____ best cheerleader at East Mount High School (a/an, the)

B.2 Can you tell me where I can find _____ math tutor to help me out? (a/an, the)

B.3 Just because she's _____ tennis player doesn't mean she's not smart. (a/an, the)

B.4 Don't worry, Kiana will show me to _____ bathroom. (a/an, the)

B.5 Logan, you are _____ worst prankster ever! (a/an, the)

An ***appositive*** is a noun or noun phrase that renames another noun right beside it. It can either be a short or long string of words. Appositives also need proper punctuation, such as commas. Some examples include:

Victor**, the best point guard on the basketball team,** carried his teammates on the court.

The only girl in the squad, Lily made sure that the boys didn't treat her any differently.

Below are some practice exercises. Circle or highlight the appositive. Also, insert where the comma(s) should go.

EXERCISE C: Appositives

C.1 Wendy the fastest girl on the track team made sure that everyone saw her finish first during the race.

C.2 Known for his wit Andrew became the valedictorian by a landslide.

C.3 Do you know Allie the prettiest girl in high school?

C.4 Mr. Richards the oldest teacher at school had enough of the boy's shenanigans in class.

C.5 Can you believe Tiffany the nerdy girl was asked out by Timmy?

Tip: Review Your Words

Why You Should Do It:

If you take the time to review your work, then you're bound to find grammatical mistakes. Most grammatical mistakes are made when students don't take the time to review their sentences because they hurry their writing and don't think about what the correct usage for each word.

How You Should Integrate It:

Before you send a text, email, or paper, make sure you look over each sentence. By doing this, you will most likely catch a mistake. Your brain is too focused on writing sentences and won't catch grammatical mistakes during that process. Sometimes, you will need to review your work more than once. You should do this if you have the extra. A few minutes spent reviewing your work will save you from making blaring mistakes.

How Often You Should Review:

You should review your work every time you write. It doesn't matter if you are talking to your best friend or sending in your personal essay for college admissions; using correct grammar *all the time* is essential. The more you practice reviewing, the better you'll become at it, too.

Conclusion

You probably are relieved to know that you knew already knew what articles and appositives are. After dealing with the difficult terminology, understanding grammar is so much easier. Until then, it confuses so many high school students—maybe that's why so many people never try to improve their grammar.

Learning what articles and appositives are and how to use them can be pretty tough, but after going through the examples and exercises, you should have a good grip on them. Go back as much as needed if you don't fully understand certain concepts. Knowing these basic blocks for great writing is very vital. One misconception can set you and your writing back a lot. So remember— take your time and review this section if needed.

CHAPTER 5

Nouns and Pronouns

Nouns and pronouns are some of the most important parts of speech; they also appear everywhere, which means you can't escape them. Almost every object (and person) is considered a noun, such as *Becky, duck, pizza, pencil, and woman.* Essentially, nouns are the main focus of sentences. Without them, sentences would lack their vigor. Pronouns substitute in place of proper nouns, typically. When you're tired of saying you friend Liam's name, you use *he* instead. Pronouns are just as relevant and vital as nouns are.

You may think you're a noun and pronoun expert already (and you may be right), but this section will help you brush up on technical definitions. It's always a great idea to review material that you think you already know inside and out because you might have forgotten a rule or reason for usage.

Take your time and go through each definition, example, and exercise to hone your skills. You may be surprised to find that you have forgotten some key terms or how to use nouns and pronouns properly.

Let's tackle nouns and pronouns, shall we?

A *noun* is a word that names a person, place, thing, or idea. Almost all words you can think of are nouns because you are constantly surrounded by them.

There are six different types of nouns: **common nouns, singular nouns, singular possessive nouns, proper nouns, plural nouns,** and **plural possessive nouns**.

- A **common noun** names general objects, such as **boat, cat,** and **necklace**.

- A **singular noun** is a noun that only refers to a single person, place, thing, or idea, such as **flag, lawyer,** and **ring**.

- A **singular possessive noun** is a singular noun that shows ownership over another object, such as **teacher's** apple, **book's** pages, and **jacket's** material.

- A **proper noun** names a specific noun, such as **Stacy, Sam,** and **John**.

- A **plural noun** is group of two or ore nouns, such as **chairs, computers,** and **kites**.

- A **plural possessive noun** is a group of two or more objects that show ownership over another object, such as **ladies'** dresses, **pumpkins'** seeds, and **friends'** clothes.

The following are some exercises. Circle the noun (whether it's a singular, plural, or proper noun etc.) in the sentence. There can be more than one in a sentence, too.

EXERCISE A: Nouns

A.1   Can you tell me where exactly the men's restroom is?

A.2   Ben's research report went mysteriously missing today after lunch.

A.3   The car that we took to the beach broke down in the way home.

A.4   Are there any more peaches in the kitchen?

A.5   Although the pie was delicious, I didn't care for the mysterious meal's ingredients.

A.6   Oliver's papers went flying everywhere in the classroom today.

A.7   Quick and silent, the rats' feet scurried along the floor.

A.8   Did you decide whether Lola or Peter are coming to dinner tonight?

A.9   You have exquisite taste, Mrs. Childers; I love your couch's fabric!

A.10   The school director's notebook went missing today, and he seems furious.

A *pronoun* is a word substituted in place of one of more nouns. It may stand for a person, place, thing, or idea. There are four types of pronouns: **personal pronouns, indefinite pronouns, demonstrative pronouns, and relative pronouns**.

- A **personal pronoun** relates to people, such as *I, you, me, mine, she, he, we, it, they, them, their, ours, myself, yourself, your,* and *theirs*.

- An **indefinite pronoun** is non-specific pronoun, such as *anybody, each, other, none, someone,* and *one*.

- A **demonstrative pronoun** shows specificity or direction, such as *this, these, that,* and *those*.

- A **relative pronoun** introduces a relative clause with words such as *who, which, whom, whose,* and *what*.

Below are some exercises that will help you understand how to use pronouns correctly. Circle or highlight the pronoun(s) in the sentence.

EXERCISE B: Pronouns

B.1 Is anybody willing to get decorate the auditorium for the school play this weekend?

B.2 I, Denise, don't think you should do that because you'll get in trouble.

B.3 Hillary, who is the new girl, got a perfect score on her U.S. history exam.

B.4 Someone came earlier and dropped off a note for you.

B.5 Are these baseball pants yours or mine?

B.6 Walter, whose mom is very strict, was grounded for three months straight.

B.7 It's always best to treat others as you'd want to be treated.

B.8 Until those clothes are cleaned, I can't leave the house.

B.9 Xavier is someone who is always there for you when you need him.

B.10 I love this university; I feel like anybody could fit in here!

Conclusion

Not as easy as you remembered, right? That's because grammar is so difficult, and nouns and pronouns are not exception. You probably forgot that there are different types of nouns and pronouns, too. But don't worry—most high school students need to review nouns and pronouns. It's easy to forget their correct usage in a world of improper grammar. However, you survived this chapter, which means you are that much closer to moving on to writing mechanics.

Hopefully this section was quite easy for you, but if not then there are additional links in the back of the book. Going through this section will help your basic fundamentals of writing even further. Once you've mastered the basics, then you'll be on your way of flawless writing that will get you into the college of your dreams. Let's now explore how to write numbers correctly in sentences.

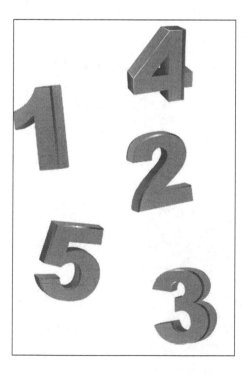

CHAPTER 6
Numbers

Unfortunately, situations occur when you need to write about numbers in sentences. You may think, *but numbers belong in mathematical expressions, not in writing.* This isn't the case sometimes. You may need to write a research report that deals with many numbers in which you need to include in the written report. This may cause a problem for you.

Although most students, or even adults, understand how to write numbers correctly, the rules still sometimes make people slip up. There are different ways to write numbers; sometimes you write them out in words, and other times you write their numerical form. It's important to understand when to use them correctly. Otherwise, it'll weaken your writing.

This section will go through every rule determining when you need to spell out the number or if you should write the numerical form instead. This may seem difficult, but the rules are actually quite simple. Study each rules and view the examples. They will help you know when to write numbers in their numerical or written form.

Whether you're writing out statistics or referring to time in general, you will need to know when to incorporate the correct written or numerical form. It's essential to know and not that difficult to learn. Below are the rules of when to use the correct form:

Rule 1: Spell out numbers at the beginning of a sentence. Never start a sentence with numbers—that's the worst mistake to make!

<u>Thirty</u> men graduated from the last police academy class.

<u>Forty</u> girls stood in line waiting for their heartthrob to appear on stage.

Below are exercises to help you practice how to spell numbers out. Rewrite the numerical form in words.

EXERCISE A: Numbers Rule 1
A.1   180 high school boys tried out for the football team this year.
A.2   20 little girls pranced onto the stage and started doing their practiced dance routine.
A.3   94 people waited in line for the new phone to come out the next day.

EXERCISE A: Numbers Rule 1

A.4   13 cars were haphazardly parked all over the place.

A.5   25 percent of the cross-country team is freshmen.

A.6   45 moms helped run the fall festival fundraiser this year.

A.7   21 puppies are for sale at the local animal shelter!

A.8   300 seniors are going to graduate from Thomas Jefferson High School this year.

EXERCISE A: Numbers Rule 1

A.9   8 new teachers were hired over the summer.

A.10   33 people now live in this neighborhood.

Rule 2: Insert a hyphen between all compound numbers. There are no exceptions to this rule. Think of the numbers are compound adjectives (which need a hyphen as well).

<u>**Fifty-three**</u> apples fell out of the bin during a farmer's market festival.

<u>**Ninety-nine**</u> percent of the time I'm right—just admit it!

Below are a few exercises for you to practice using hyphens in between compound numbers. Rewrite the sentence with the inserted hyphen.

EXERCISE B: Numbers Rule 2

B.1   Sixty two percent of girls in this high school have ambitions for getting into Ivy League schools.

B.2   Twenty one eggs were used for this recipe.

B.3   Forty six championship awards are polished weekly in the awards room.

EXERCISE B: Numbers Rule 2
B.4   Eighty eight families have donated to this school over the years.
B.5   Fifty two little leaguers stormed onto the field after the tournament was over.
B.6   Thirty seven flower arrangements were ordered this morning!
B.7   Forty three students were added to the 2017 freshmen class.
B.8   Seventy eight percent of the students passed the history exam.

EXERCISE B: Numbers Rule 2

B.9 Ninety two authors were born and raised in this state.

B.10 Twenty three teachers are up for public school award nominations.

Rule 3: Write out decades in numerals. Spelling out the decade is too much and confuses readers.

In the **1920s**, flappers were considered scandalous but now they are celebrated.

My father was born sometime in the **1960s**.

Below are a few exercises to practice with. Convert the written-out form of each decade to the numeral form.

EXERCISE C: Numbers Rule 3

C.1 In nineteen sixty-nine, my father was born in Indianapolis.

EXERCISE C: Numbers Rule 3

C.2   Email and the Internet took over the business world in the early two thousand's.

C.3   In the late seventeen hundreds, Jane Austen wrote the some of the best novels in the English language.

C.4   Did you know that America was very prosperous in the eighteen hundreds?

C.5   In the nineteen hundreds, industrialization soon took over the economy.

Rule 4: Write out shortened decade figures. Sometimes, you can spell them out, but it's generally accepted to use their numerical form.

Disco took over the entire nation in the **'70s**.

The **'40s** was a hard time for peace, stability, and prosperity because of World War II.

Below are some exercises to practice with. Insert the comma correctly on the decade.

EXERCISE D: Numbers Rule 4

D.1   The Cold War erupted in the 50s and caused the United States and the USSR to have conflict.

D.2   The Roaring 20s was a time of excessive drinking, dancing, and frivolous fun.

D.3   In the 90s, the Internet was invented and started becoming useful for businesses.

D.4   Did you know that America's economy was pretty good in the 40s?

D.5   Please re-do your hair; you look like you should stepped out of an 80s flick.

Rule 5: When spelling out decades, don't capitalize them. (There is no exception to this rule.)

The **nineties** was a time when boy bands and pop music was all the rage.

Hippies, psychedelic music, and drugs took over the youthful generation in the **sixties**.

Below are some exercises to practice with. Determine whether the sentence is correct or incorrect by circling the answer.

EXERCISE E: Numbers Rule 5

E.1 In the mid-seventies, civil rights were fought across the country. (correct, incorrect)

E.2 I wished I had lived in the Eighties. (correct, incorrect)

E.3 Walt Disney opened Disney World in the 70s. (correct, incorrect)

E.4 In '52, my grandparents met for the first time. (correct, incorrect)

E.5 The Thirties was a difficult time for Americans. (correct, incorrect)

Rule 6: Hyphenate all written-out fractions. (Remember the compound adjective rule.)

About **two-thirds** of all high school dropouts are due to poor living conditions.

There are about **three-fourths** of girls who attend this high school now.

The exercises below will help you practice writing out fractions. Rewrite the fractions from their numerical form into their written form.

EXERCISE F: Numbers Rule 6
F.1   I need a 2/3 cup of sugar for this cookie recipe.
F.2   The principal said that my skirt needs to be 3/5 of an inch past my knee.
F.3   About 1/3 of the basketball team flunked their math exam.
F.4   About 5/6 of the band is made up of girls.
F.5   Can you tell that only ¼ of this room is filled up?

Rule 7: When talking about 12:00 a.m. or 12:00 p.m., it's best to use *noon* or *midnight*. It makes writing so much easier on you and the reader.

Is our first exam at **noon** tomorrow?

I can never fall asleep until at least **midnight**.

Below are some practice exercises to use. Fill in the blank with *noon* or *midnight*.

EXERCISE G: Numbers Rule 7

G.1 Do you want to meet up around _____ for coffee? (noon, midnight)

G.2 Let's go stargazing at _____! (noon, midnight)

G.3 Can you make sure that Sally makes it to dance practice at _____ on Saturday? (noon, midnight)

G.4 At _____, Kate and Georgia decided to go for a bike ride. (noon, midnight)

G.5 I couldn't fall asleep until _____, and today I'm exhausted. (noon, midnight)

Rule 8: Write out *million* and *billion* instead of using their numerical forms.

I can think of a **million** reasons why you should stay in high school.

Did you hear that Megan's father makes $2.3 million dollars a year?

Below are some exercises to practice with. Convert the numerical form to written-out form.

EXERCISE H: Numbers Rule 8
H.1   Man, what I would do with $1,000,000!
H.2   Can you believe that Mark Zuckerberg is worth $3,000,000,000?
H.3   That house must be worth at least $8,000,000.

Rule 9: Write decimals using figures.

I don't think **2.56** is the correct answer for this math problem.

I think everybody knows that the formula of pi starts with **3.14**.

Below are some exercises to practice with. Determine whether the sentence is correct or incorrect.

EXERCISE I: Numbers Rule 9

I.1   About 12.9 percent of the class voted for a new president. (correct, incorrect)

I.2   There is an eight point two percent chance that I will not go to dinner tonight. (correct, incorrect)

I.3   Can you believe that 84.3 percent of the alumni gives donations on a regular basis? (correct, incorrect)

Conclusion

You survived Chapter 4—congratulations. It wasn't as hard as you imagined, right? Although you don't need to write numbers in everyday writing, it's still important to understand how to write them correctly. If you're having trouble with a few rules, go back through this chapter and study each example. The more you spend time on each rule, the better you'll understand it, guaranteed.

Writing numbers correctly can be very tricky. After working through this chapter, hopefully you feel confident about writing any small or large numbers in their written or numerical form. If you're still having difficulties, refer to the additional links at the end of the book. Remember—the more you practice, the more you'll transform into an incredible, confident writer.

Let's move onto an essential element—prepositions.

"A preposition is a terrible thing to end a sentence with."

- WINSTON S. CHURCHILL

CHAPTER 7
Prepositions

Prepositions can be considered the descriptive additions to sentences. They explain what the subject and verb are acting on in the sentence. Most people forget that prepositions are used very often in conversation and writing, so it's important to understand their meaning. Without prepositions and prepositional phrases, sentences would be bland and remain ambiguous for the reader.

Jamie ran.

Jamie ran **behind the wall**.

Prepositions trip high school students up all the time. They were never fully expounded on in the classroom, so they can cause difficulty for certain students. This section breaks down what prepositions are, what they look like in a sentence, and give you a chance to identify them in sentences. Make sure you understand this section—it's a basic fundamental for improving your overall writing.

A **preposition** presents a noun, pronoun, phrase or clause functioning in the sentence as a noun. The word (or word group) that it introduces is its *object*. A *prepositional phrase* includes a preposition with other modifiers that create a descriptive phrase. There are three functions that the preposition serves.

Preposition + Noun/Pronoun = Object of Preposition

- The preposition never stands alone: There is always a subject or object connected to the preposition. Some examples include:

  They received an assignment **from** Mrs. Tillman describing the requirements.

  Can you see what's **underneath** the piles of scattered papers?

- **Prepositions can have more than one object:** There isn't a rule that says that the preposition in a given sentence only has one object; beware of two or more objects in certain sentences (especially in the exercises below).

  You can see the organism **under** the *microscope* and *magnifier*.

  | ⇧ | ⇧ | ⇧ |
  | PREPOSITION | OBJECT | OBJECT |

  Have you found my favorite book **beside** the *bed table* or *dresser*?

- **Some prepositions have different modifiers:** Just like prepositions can have more than one object, they also can have multiple modifiers.

  The bat and baseball is lying **against** the sliding glass doors.

  Margaret and Mandy are walking **toward** the river.

Here is a list of common prepositions that you may use on a daily basis or plan to use in the future. (These include and aren't limited to the only prepositions.)

- Under
- To
- From
- About
- Along
- Across
- Aboard
- Around
- At
- Upon
- Before
- Beside
- Above
- Between
- Beyond
- After

- By
- Down
- During
- Within
- Toward
- In
- Throughout
- Underneath
- Without
- Except
- For
- Since
- Until
- Over
- Behind
- Beneath

- Against
- Below
- Off
- Among
- With
- Through
- Up
- Past
- On
- Of
- Like
- Into
- By
- Near
- Onto
- Opposite

The following are exercises to practice identifying prepositions in the sentence. Circle the preposition(s) in the sentence and underline the object(s) as well. Check your answers in the back of the book if you feel unsure about the accuracy of your answers.

EXERCISE A: Prepositions

A.1 Rachael and her three younger siblings ran along the edge of the neighborhood.

A.2 Is there a way that you can work through this pile of laundry in the afternoon?

A.3 The homecoming queen was lost in the crowd among fans and students.

A.4 We love to make popsicles and go swimming during the summer.

A.5 I believe Gina lives near the farmer's market and duck pond in Richmond.

A.6 From the stage, the singer leapt into the enthusiastic crowd.

A.7 There is this beautiful path with wild flowers and blueberries across the field.

A.8 With extra sleep and medicine, Nora kicked her cold and is feeling much better.

A.9 If you keep going left and past the cemetery, you'll find Ben's house.

A.10 Even though we had limited light and supplies, we trudged through the thick trees and bushes.

Conclusion

Once again, you survived another chapter. Now prepositions don't look as scary, right? If anything, you probably now have a newfound appreciation for them; they make sentences so much better. After relearning prepositions and prepositional phrases, you may feel like you can conquer any other grammar basic—and you're right.

At first, defining and identifying prepositions may intimidate you because you haven't learned their technical meaning and use since elementary school. After going through the definition, examples, and exercises, hopefully you've become a master of prepositions. If you're still struggling with how to use them or identify them in sentences, go back and look over their definitions. Answers to exercises and additional links can be found at the end of the book for more help and exercises to practice with.

Let's tackle the next chapter—verbs.

- RICHARD MITCHELL

CHAPTER 8

Verbs

You probably looked at this chapter's titles and thought, *why do I need to review verbs? That's for elementary kids.* Perhaps, you're right. But reviewing verbs is an essential building block of flawless writing. You need to understand their definition and what purpose they serve in a sentence. There may be some rules that you have forgotten about since you first learned what a verb is.

Verb tenses are one of the trickiest parts of speech, especially in the English language. With so many exceptions to rules, it's hard to master verbs and their tenses. This chapter will give you a brief but thorough review of verbs and how to use them. ***This is one of the most important sections in this book.*** Take the time to go through each rule, so you fully understand what verbs are and what function they serve. Even if you're a verb expert, review the material so you fully understand each rule and definition.

A **verb** is a word that expresses an action or helps complete a sentence. There are three types of verbs: action, linking, and irregular. (Using irregular verbs is a very complicated matter, so you won't go over that material until the next chapter.)

There is also one simple rule to remember: **Every sentence *must* have a verb.** There's no escaping it. Verbs are vital to making sentences have purpose and meaning, so it's important to know the correct form.

> He **drove** the speedy sports car.
>
> She **has been** feeling ill.

You may think it's fairly simple to identify and use verbs, but you may have trouble recognizing and knowing all five tenses of verbs: **infinitive, simple present, simple past, past participle,** and **present participle**.

INFINITIVE	SIMPLE PRESENT	SIMPLE PAST	PAST PARTICIPLE	PRESENT PARTICIPLE
To laugh	Laugh(s)	Laughed	Laughed	Laughing
To edit	Edit(s)	Edited	Edited	Editing
To play	Play(s)	Played	Played	Playing

Action Verbs, as their name depicts, show action, such as mental or physical action.

> Kylie **drilled** a hole into the piece of wood to put a string through it.
>
> Iron Man **punched** the villain when he tried to get away.
>
> Natalie **planned** out every detail in her head.

It's very important to know a plethora of action verbs because they make sentences stronger. Some action verbs, such as *acquired, anticipated, channeled, coached, compared, delivered, drafted, edited, explored, focused, managed,* and *measured*. At the end of the book is a list of action verbs. Memorize these verbs and practice using them in everyday conversation and writing.

The following are exercises to practice using action verbs. Simply circle the action verb given in the sentence.

EXERCISE A: Action Verbs

A.1   Professor X, from the X-Men movies, combats with his arch-nemesis at the end of the series.

A.2   Suffering from insomnia, the student slept through her morning classes.

A.3   Janice slapped John in the face when he stood her up on their date.

A.4   He angered me when he said that my paper was lousy.

A.5   Whether or not it's right, Naomi kissed Dick in the parking lot after school.

Linking verbs   make a statement by connecting the subject of the sentence with a word that describes or explains. Typically, you use linking verbs in most sentences because they link the subject to the predicate. Below is a linking verb formula:

Subject + Linking Verbs + Predicate

The Orion belt **is** a series of stars that appear in the sky at night.

Are my children behaving properly in school?

Some linking verbs include *is, are, sound, appear, smell, felt, became,* and *has been.* Most verbs are linking verbs and are a part of everyday life.

Below are exercises to practice identifying linking verbs. Circle the linking verb in the sentence, underline the subject, and double underline the predicate.

EXERCISE B: Linking Verbs

B.1 During the winter in the northeast, the weather is sometimes frigid and unbearable to locals and visitors.

B.2 I felt like my English teacher didn't notice how much effort I put into my personal essay.

B.3 It has been a crazy day filled with washing the car, mowing the lawn, and paying the bills.

B.4 Whether it's true or not, the pep band sounds like it hasn't practiced in the off-season.

B.5 When the caterpillar breaks from its cocoon, it becomes a magnificent butterfly.

Conclusion

Verbs make sentences come alive. If used improperly, they ruin sentences. Remember—a sentence isn't a sentence without a verb, so you can't avoid using verbs in conversation or writing. It's important to use the correct tense because you will speak or write awkward sentences that don't make sense. So take your time reviewing each definition!

After working through each exercise and viewing each example, identifying and using verbs properly should be easier for you. Verbs aren't too difficult to understand, so hopefully this chapter was a great review for you. If you are still having some difficulties, there are some additional links located at the end of the book for your use. The next chapter will discuss irregular verbs and their unusual tense changes.

Let's move on.

"Perfect grammar--persistent, continuous, sustained--is the fourth dimension, so to speak: many have sought it, but none has found it."

- MARK TWAIN

CHAPTER 9
Irregular Verbs

Yes, this chapter is dedicated solely to irregular verbs. Why? Because they're a complicated subsection of verbs and need to be broken down further. There are so many irregular verbs that pop up in everyday conversation, and most people use the wrong tense when they speak or write. In order to avoid this mistake, look over irregular verbs and their definition.

This chapter will explain what irregular verbs are and what purpose they serve. Verbs can make or break your sentence, so it's very important that you understand this section. Answers are provided at the end of this guide for reference. Also, additional links and websites are provided in the back of this book for help with irregular verbs.

Irregular verbs change into unusual forms compared to regular verbs. It's difficult to remember which tense it switches to; that's why so many people struggle with using the correct form.

Did you **write** about The Beatles or Bob Dylan?

I **wrote** about Bob Dylan and his rise to fame in the music world.

Ginny **has written** a couple of essays on music legends.

It's almost impossible to memorize every single irregular verb, so using them in conversation and writing will help you learn them better. The following is a chart of irregular verbs in their base form, past simple form, and past participle form.

BASE FORM	PAST SIMPLE	PAST PARTICIPLE
Awake	Awoke	Has/Have Awoken
Be	Was, Were	Has/Have Been
Become	Became	Has/Have Become
Begin	Began	Has/Have Begun
Blow	Blew	Has/Have Blown
Break	Broke	Has/Have Broken
Buy	Bought	Has/Have Bought
Come	Came	Has/Have Come
Draw	Drew	Has/Have Drawn
Drink	Drank	Has/Have Drunk
Hang	Hung	Has/Have Hung
Lay	Laid	Has/Have Laid
Sing	Sang	Has/Have Sung
Tear	Tore	Has/Have Torn
Write	Wrote	Has/Have Written
Feel	Felt	Has/Have Felt

Many students struggle with using the correct form of irregular verb, but it's such an easy mistake to fix. There are tons of resources online (and in this book) that will help you remember when to use the correct form. Using incorrect irregular verbs are red flags for teachers, potential employers and other adults who are considering you for a position somewhere. Make sure you know which forms to use and when.

The following are exercises to help you use irregular verbs properly. Circle or insert the correct form into the sentence.

EXERCISE A: Irregular Verbs

A.1 Have you _____ our school's alma mater during a sporting event? (sang, sung)

A.2 Do you usually _____ here or to the other Italian restaurant down the street? (came, come)

A.3 Judy and Florence _____ coming down from North Dakota during the summer in a few months. (is, are)

A.4 Warren _____ that Derek was being too competitive during swimming practice. (feel, felt)

A.5 George _____ his new puppy in his bed so he could get used to the new environment. (lay, laid)

A.6 It's a false theory to think that you instantaneously _____ an adult once you graduate high school and start college (become, became).

A.7 How much water have you _____ today? It's very important to drink often. (drank, drunk)

A.8 Have you _____ this type of burger yet? If you haven't, then you need to _____ it soon. (eaten, ate) (ate, eat)

A.9 Pippa, a foreign exchange student, has _____ me a map of her hometown village in Lithuania. (drew, drawn)

A.10 There is a _____ in my new uniform, and I can't fix it. (tore, tear)

Conclusion

Irregular verbs aren't too difficult to master if you brush up on the unusual form changes, and you can use them correctly if you take the time to practice using their different forms. Unfortunately, there are many irregular verbs that are used on a daily basis, so you can't avoid them altogether. Take the time to look over the examples and chart of irregular verbs to refresh your memory.

With practice, you will learn and use them correctly. If you still struggle with them, it's okay. Most people do. There are additional links in the back of the book if you would like more practice exercises to work on. If you keep practicing, then you'll eventually use them correctly.

CHAPTER 10
Subject-Verb Agreement

Subject-verb agreement is an essential rule to remember; otherwise, it'll ruin your sentence. However, most people use the wrong verb with a singular or plural subject all the time. It's a common mistake because most people use the wrong word in daily conversation. By reviewing this rule and examining the examples below, you will no longer struggle with subject-verb agreement.

Most high school students also struggle with subject-verb agreement because sometimes the correct verb sounds weird with the singular or plural subject. This is very important because your sentence will self-destruct if the sentence's subject and verb don't agree. This chapter breaks down the complicated rule and provides examples of how the subject and verb are supposed to coincide. Take your time as you go through the examples and exercises so you fully understand the concept.

Every sentence has two vital parts: the **subject** and the **predicate**. The subject of the sentence is the part about which something is being said.

> **Kelly** is applying to Princeton in hopes of being a legacy after her father and mother.
> **The birds** flew high in the sky in a "V" formation.

There are also two different kinds of subjects, too: **simple subject** and **complete subject**. A simple subject is a one-word (or main) subject, such as *teachers, fish, lemon, Sara,* and *America.* The complete subject consists of a main word and modifiers, such as *new, nervous teachers; greasy, pepperoni pizza; little, frail lamb;* and *brave, young soldier.*

After quickly refreshing your mind about what a subject is and previously relearning what a verb is in the last chapter, there are a few rules to go over below.

1. When the subject of a sentence is composed of two or more nouns or pronouns connected by *and,* use a verb.

   Molly and **her teammates** *are* preparing for their game.
   The dog and **its companions** *are* roaming around the trash bins.

2. When two or more singular nouns or pronouns are connected by *or* or *nor,* use a singular verb.

   The **math** or **history** exam *is* tomorrow.
   Do you know if **Jake** nor **Hank** *is* working right now?

3. When a compound subject contains both a singular and plural noun/pronoun joined by *or* or *nor,* the verb should agree with the part of the subject that is nearer the verb.

   Molly or **her friends** *run* every day.
   Her friends or **Molly** *runs* every day.

4. Don't be tricked by a phrase that comes between the subject and verb. The verb agrees with the subject, not with a noun or pronoun in the phrase.

One of the runners *is* injured.

The students who listen to the teacher *are* few.

The class president, as well as his fellow classmates, *is* anxious about the principal's opinion.

5. The words *each, each one, either, neither, everyone, everybody, anybody, anyone, nobody, somebody, someone* and *no one* are considered singular and require a singular verb.

Each of these test results *is* bad.

Everybody *loves* the mascot.

6. Collective nouns, such as *group, team, committee, class*, and *family*, are words that imply more than one person but are considered singular and need a singular verb.

The committee *determines* the new set of rules.

The group *is* in charge of homecoming this year.

7. Expressions, such as *with, together with, including, accompanied by, in addition to,* or *as well,* don't change the number of the subject.

The principal, **accompanied by** the teacher, is walking in the auditorium.

In addition to joining the debate team, Josie works at the diner and is the president of the club soccer team.

The following are exercises for you to practice using correct subject-verb agreement. Circle or insert the correct word in the sentence.

EXERCISE A: Subject-Verb Agreement

A.1 The group of women, even though they come from different backgrounds, _____ the best fundraisers and raise so much money for different local non-profit organizations. (plan, plans)

A.2 The gymnast, accompanied by trainers, _____ lying on the floor after falling from the bar. (is, are)

A.3 Each of us _____ going to the strawberry festival this weekend but at different times. (are, is)

A.4 One of the scouts _____ looking at a few baseball players on our high school team. (is, are)

A.5 Either Billy or Timmy _____ going away this weekend to look at some potential colleges. (is, are)

A.6 His friends or Jimmy _____ for the new band that formed a few months ago. (sings, sing)

A.7 Everybody _____ happy with their ACT and SAT scores, but I'm very unsatisfied. (are, is)

A.8 In Greek mythology, Zeus and Hera _____ the parents of many gods and goddesses. (is, are)

A.9 Although mistakes have been made, the committee _____ still attempting to make the next couple of events run more smoothly. (are, is)

A.10 Some of these school outfits _____ not suitable for the winter time, especially during P.E. (is, are)

Conclusion

One of the most common grammatical errors, the subject-verb agreement isn't too hard to if you practice usually the correct verb form. Most people, especially high school students, accidently use a plural verb form instead of a singular form in daily conversation, which leads to mistakes in written forms. If you are still struggling with subject-verb agreement, there is additional links provided in the back for you.

Congratulations—you've survived each grammar chapter. Now you are ready to tackle writing mechanics that will further improve your writing abilities. Part 2 isn't quite as boring or difficult as Part 1, but you may struggle with certain chapters and exercises. As frequently stated, work through each concept at a slow pace so you fully understand each rule and correct usage.

PART 2
Writing Mechanics

Part 2 takes all the basic fundamentals that you learned in Part One and applies them into writing mechanics. If you haven't fully understood each grammar rule in the previous sections, then go back and work through each chapter. In order to understand the difficulties of writing mechanics, then you must be founded in the basics.

This section will take you through writing mechanics that will improve your writing and prepare you for the writing process. There is a plethora of explanations, examples, and exercises to work through. If you are having with certain chapters or mechanics, go back over them at a slow pace and spend as much time practicing and understanding each concept as much as you need to. Every student learns at his or her own pace; don't rush through if that's not your type of learning style. Let's dive into the essential elements of writing, shall we?

CHAPTER 11
The Sentence Breakdown

The sentence breakdown: an essential way to understand what a sentence consists of and what makes them great. This chapter will briefly explain what makes a sentence good. Sometimes, simple sentences are considered better than long, complex sentences. Why? Because they don't trip the reader up. The fewer the words you use, the better the sentence.

Although Part One already went through each part of speech, this chapter breaks down the sentence as a collective whole. In order to write eloquent, brief sentences instead of sloppy ones, you need to review what elements create a great sentence.

All great writing begins with the sentence. Just like good grammar skills create good sentences, good sentences create good writing. (That just blew your mind right then, didn't it?) Flawless writing is created by correct and essential building blocks (i.e. grammar, sentences, and paragraphs), so breaking down the sentence is the next building clock to conquer.

Let's explore the sentence, shall we?

A *sentence* is essentially a group of words that expresses a thought. Every sentence must have a subject, verb, and predicate. Of course, reviewing what a sentence is seems very senseless, but understanding what a sentence consists of will help you write great, flawless sentences. Below are the different types of sentences explained.

A *simple sentence* is a sentence consisting of only one clause, with a single subject and predicate. This type of sentence is the most basic form, being very succinct and lacking description.

However, simple sentences are considered the best sentence to write. Great writers, like Ernest Hemingway, believed that simple, short sentences make up the best type of writing. Below are examples:

The Lord of the Rings trilogy is one of the best-selling science-fiction series ever.

The fantasy football league is very popular in America.

Jonah has stopped by the house to show us his new pet snake.

Below are exercises where you can create your own simple sentence. A few words are offered in each exercise, so feel free to use them and write your own sentence. Examples of simple sentences are provided in the back of the book.

EXERCISE A: Simple Sentence
A.1 (sledding, Abby, is)

EXERCISE A: Simple Sentence

A.2　(were, Bobby, Dennis, eating)

A.3　(wrote, Lily, love letter)

A.4　(Ian, laundry, folds)

A.5　(knows, Casey, Chinese)

A ***compound sentence*** is a sentence with more than one subject or predicate. Essentially, more than one idea, thought, or subject is combined into one sentence instead of two.

Gwen is going to the most prestigious art camp this summer, and Greg is attending the national debate team conference in California.

Baseball isn't as popular now as it was back then, but football increases popularity each year.

I plan on studying engineering in college, and Fred wants to study architecture.

Below are exercises where you will create your own compound sentence. Two subjects and a verb will be given. Using those words, write your own unique compound sentence. Examples of compound sentences are provided in the answer section.

EXERCISE B: Compound Sentence
B.1   (soccer, football, is)
B.2   (pizza, salad, is)
B.3   (Led Zeppelin, Black Sabbath, plays)

EXERCISE B: Compound Sentence

B.4 (sofa, chair, sits)

B.5 (gym, treadmill, is)

A *complex sentence* is a sentence containing a subordinate clause or clauses. Complex sentences are very common, but most people, especially students, struggle writing great complex sentences without little to none grammatical errors in them.

> Despite having little preparation beforehand, Rebecca scored exceedingly well on each Advanced Placement tests in May.
>
> Callie and Dave first met in high school during gym class when Dave fell on his face.
>
> Whenever the leaves fall, I anticipate the cool, autumn nights that follow.

Below are exercises to practice writing error-free complex sentences. A subject, verb, and preposition are given in each exercise. Create your own complex sentences with the given words. There are guided answers provided in the back of the book if you are unsure whether your sentence is correct.

EXERCISE C: Complex Sentence
C.1   (apple pie, coffee, after)
C.2   (despite, Kevin, Mindy)
C.3   (through, trees, bushes)
C.4   (awards, prizes, behind)
C.5   (before, quill, ink)

There are four kinds of sentences that you should understand and know when to use them. Different writing styles, such as when writing an essay, email, recommendation letter, or research report, call for certain types of sentences.

Below are descriptions of four types of sentences: declarative, interrogative, exclamatory, and imperative sentences.

A *declarative sentence* makes a statement and typically uses a period for punctuation. Most common types of sentences are declarative.

> Fly fishing may seem like a boring sport but it's quite exhilarating.
>
> Some of our farm animals include horses, cows, chickens, goats, donkeys, and pigs.
>
> Mr. Lyons has won multiple awards for his outstanding lectures and discussions.

An *interrogatory sentence* is a sentence that has or conveys the force of a question. In more common terms, it is a question in the form of a sentence.

> Do you know where the island of St. Maarten is on the map?
>
> Can you think of a more perfect evening than tonight?
>
> What did Shanna, Hillary, and Jenny plan for their winter vacations?

An *exclamatory sentence* is a sentence that depicts emotion or strong feeling. Very few sentences are exclamatory, and some authors are strongly against their use.

> Oh my goodness, I've been waiting for this moment for quite sometime!
>
> You need to come see what's over here, Ms. Jackson!
>
> I can't believe that Carrie Wilson won the Miss Florida pageant!

An *imperative sentence* is a sentence that gives an authoritative command of great importance. Generally, you don't use imperative sentences in written formats.

Jordan, please come over here and pick up the clothes, books, and papers.

Fill out these applications and turn in the rest of the documents by the end of the day.

Complete your high school career well, and you will get into the college of dreams.

Below are exercises to help you determine when a sentence is declarative, exclamatory, imperative, or interrogative. Circle the correct answer. Answers are provided in the back of the book.

EXERCISE D: Declarative, Exclamatory, Imperative, Interrogative

D.1 I love how relaxing the last day of school is for the students, faculty, and staff! (declarative, imperative, interrogative, exclamatory)

D.2 Can you direct me to the nearest tourist information center, please? (declarative, imperative, interrogative, exclamatory)

D.3 If you love thrilling rides, Ohio, by far, has the best rollercoasters in the country. (declarative, imperative, interrogative, exclamatory)

D.4 Grab the bucket full of soap and water then wipe down every surface in the store before you close up for the day. (declarative, imperative, interrogative, exclamatory)

D.5 Run at a fast speed toward the target, plant down the pole, then jump over without hitting the other pole. (declarative, imperative, interrogative, exclamatory)

EXERCISE D: Declarative, Exclamatory, Imperative, Interrogative

D.6 I can't believe I scored free tickets to go see John Mayer in concert this Saturday! (declarative, imperative, interrogative, exclamatory)

D.7 What other choices do I have after high school besides attending college or working abroad? (declarative, imperative, interrogative, exclamatory)

D.8 I think January and February are definitely in the coldest months out of the year. (declarative, imperative, interrogative, exclamatory)

D.9 Please hand these documents to Mr. Hanson and take these boxes to Ms. Jennings, too. (declarative, imperative, interrogative, exclamatory)

D.10 Oh my goodness, Neil won the grand prize and is going to Hawaii for two weeks! (declarative, imperative, interrogative, exclamatory)

Conclusion

The sentence breakdown wasn't so bad, right? Learning about the different types of sentences will give you, the writer, an advantage because you will understand when to use certain types of sentences in different writing formats. Now you are a sentence conqueror—pat yourself on the back.

After learning the building blocks of grammar, it's important to understand the different types of sentences and how to write great ones. Just like great grammar creates great sentences, great sentences create great writing. Hopefully this chapter was helpful for you. If you are still struggling with the basics of the sentence, there are additional links provided in the back of the book. Now, onto the rest of writing mechanics.

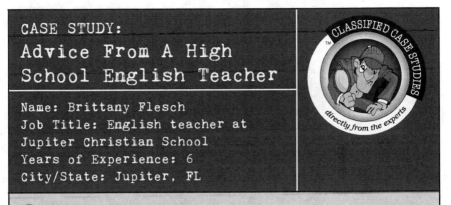

CASE STUDY:
Advice From A High School English Teacher

Name: Brittany Flesch
Job Title: English teacher at Jupiter Christian School
Years of Experience: 6
City/State: Jupiter, FL

Q What are some of the most common grammar and writing mistakes you've seen?

The misuse of whether/weather; lose/loose; their/there/they're; then/than; affect/effect happens often. Also, comma rules, such as splitting subject and verb.

Ex: Another side of the spectrum, shows the worst possible scenario of how the world could be.

Q How do you try to improve/teach students how to use better grammar and writing styles?

I conduct writing workshops which focus on 1 to 2 grammar rules, requiring rote memorization of rule, practicing and assessing (repetition), applying rule within writing assignments. I also use examples from Student's Writing Grammar Boot Camp: fun, group competition of learning, teaching, and practicing grammar rules and skills.

Q What do you recommend for students to do in order to improve on their own?

I recommend additional practice exercises of rule(s) learned in class: repetition, repetition, repetition! Also, finding examples of misuse in newspapers, blogs, television, movies, etc. helps, too.

Q Why is it important for students (especially in high school) to have good grammar and writing skills?

It's important to improve critical thinking and for varied, complex and logical communication that meets professional work and communication standards.

Q Any additional advice for students?

Practicing the art of writing may not make you perfect, but it does make you a better communicator, thinker, and writer. It's a skill that must be taught, learned, practice, and utilized, in order to be achieved and mastered!

CHAPTER 12

Punctuation and Common Phrasal Verbs

This chapter delves in between grammar and writing mechanics. Punctuation, phrasal verbs, and idioms help compose great sentences—only if you use them correctly. It's hard to use them correctly if you don't remember their technical definition or know how to use them in general. Let's get started and dive into chapter.

Punctuation

Punctuation consists of marks, such as period, comma, exclamation point, and parentheses that are used in writing to separate sentences and their elements and to clarify meaning. Most high school students struggle with punctuation and, quite frankly, don't believe that it's important to always use correctly. However, punctuation dictates the entire meaning of the sentence. Look below for some examples:

Let's eat, grandma!

Let's eat grandma!

Henry, come grab this Frisbee and play with your brother.

Henry, come grab this Frisbee and play with your brother!

Without correct punctuation, a sentence is weakened and lacks purpose. In order to master the use of punctuation, let's take a brief review over different types of punctuation. Each type also has examples and exercises to practice with.

A **period** (.) is a punctuation mark used at the end of the sentence. This is the most commonly used punctuation mark to end sentences.

> Mrs. Lehman and Mr. Shannon are the new athletic coaches that were just hired.
>
> I hope I have enough school supplies to last me the entire year.
>
> The new bus route makes it much easier for me to get to my first class on time.

An **exclamation point** (!) is a punctuation mark that indicates an ejaculated expression of feeling, such as happiness, surprise, anger, or bewilderment. Some writers believe that exclamation points should rarely be used because they take away the emphasis of the sentence. However, it's your choice when to use exclamation points.

> I can't imagine going to college without you, Abigail!
>
> The Washington Redskins won the game within the last minute of the fourth quarter!
>
> I'm going to see my favorite musician play live music in a couple of months!

The following are exercises that will help you remember when to use a period or exclamation point at the end of the sentence. Fill in the blank with a period or exclamation point. Answers are given in the end of the book.

EXERCISE A: Punctuation

A.1 When talking about switching high schools, my mom gets very upset_

A.2 I won the scholarship for being the female athlete of the year at my high school___

A.3 My favorite dish that I eat every year at Thanksgiving is mashed potatoes and gravy_

A.4 Isabelle, come look at the October issue of Cosmopolitan_

A.5 Penelope was the wife of Odysseus in the Iliad and Odyssey_

A.6 Winston, the school's bulldog mascot, pranced out onto the field before kick-off_

A.7 Erica is coming home this Saturday from her first semester in college_

A.8 After going to the farmer's market, I'll never buy vegetables from the store every again_

A.9 I feel great after drinking a couple of espresso shots this morning_

A.10 Hillary bought a couple of candles from the semi-annual sale last week_

A *colon* (:) is a punctuation mark that either introduces a quotation or list of items, or separates two clauses in which the latter elaborates on the first clause. You should only use a colon in very few cases because it's better to use a period.

There are three things you need in order to succeed: perseverance, patience, and hard work.

Oliver, these are the four colors you need: red, yellow, green, and blue.

Be aware: you will flunk the final if you don't start studying now.

Colons are generally more acceptable in general writing than other types of punctuations. Most great writers and scholars believe that periods should only be used in daily writing. However, colons are often used in scientific reports or essays because they depict a cause and effect.

A **semicolon is** a punctuation mark (;) indicating a pause, typically between two main clauses, that is more pronounced than that indicated by a comma. As stated before, use semicolons a little as possible. It's better to use two sentences instead of trying two thoughts into one. Most students, and adults, don't know how to properly use a semicolon.

I didn't know that pickles were pickled cucumbers; I just found that out last year.

My favorite part of Christmas is seeing all my relatives; I only get to see them once a year.

Quinn, Reggie's new puppy, is a golden retriever; he follows him around everywhere.

The following are exercises that will help you learn where and when to use either a colon or semicolon. Circle the correct punctuation in each sentence. Answers are provided in the back of the guide if you need to double-check your answers.

EXERCISE B: Colon or Semicolon

B.1 Please have these various items ready in your hand_ your passport, driver's license and ticket. (; or :)

B.2 Heed Mrs. Carlson's warning_ don't go into that house unless you want to get hurt. (; or :)

B.3 Let me help you with that_ it looks like that's too heavy for you to carry all by yourself. (; or :)

B.4 Aaron told me that you're thinking of applying to some Ivy league schools__ let me offer you some good advice about admissions. (; or :)

B.5 There are only a few requirements for this job_ have adequate typing skills, conversation skills, and a good attitude. (; or :)

B.6 Let me repeat the question again_ what were you doing while skipping class? (; or :)

B.7 Help Hallie with the door_ she is carrying a lot of stuff right now. (; or :)

B.8 By the way, Glenn is taking the trash out right now_ he can take yours for you if you would like him to. (; or :)

B.9 Just trust me on this one_ you'll want to go to this concert. (; or :)

B.10 I can't wait to see how the baby room will turn out_ I'm sure it's going to look so cute! (; or :)

If you had trouble with some of the exercises, make sure you go through the examples and definitions again.

Parentheses are a pair of round brackets ( ) used to mark off a parenthetical word or phrase. Although most high school students don't usually use parentheses in daily writing, but it's good to understand how to properly use it.

> You can buy your books for a cheaper price at that store (or at least I did).
>
> Zeus (also known as Jupiter) was the most powerful god.
>
> Can Jen (or Candace) please cover my shift for next Thursday night?

The following are exercises to help you understand when and where to use parentheses. Insert the parentheses correctly into the sentence. Answers are provided in the back of the guide for reference.

EXERCISE C: Parentheses

C.1 Paulina and also Jack are going to the new play tonight in downtown.

C.2 Zelda also known as the crazy cat lady adopted two more cats this morning

C.3 If you can get to the game on time or even if you're late, please help out at the concessions stand for me.

C.4 What are you going to do with these wall decorations or the window treatments lying on the floor?

C.5 Other than staying up until 4 a.m. and consuming way too much caffeine, the project turned out well!

C.6 Whether you go or don't go, I will be there around 4 p.m. this afternoon.

C.7 Katie also known as the dragon slayer beats all her guy friends at video games.

C.8 I packed all the boxes and maybe some other bags in the car to take to the garage sale tomorrow morning.

C.9 During the latter portion of the exam, I think I messed up my answers or maybe it was in the beginning.

C.10 Until an hour ago or maybe it was earlier than that, I didn't know that I am the valedictorian of my class when we graduate!

Sometimes, parentheses aren't needed when commas can substitute in their place. Remember to use parentheses when there is an interjection or random thought inserted into the sentence. Let's move on to the next punctuation.

A ***comma*** is a punctuation mark (,) indicating a pause between parts of a sentence. It is also used to separate items in a list and to mark the place of thousands in a large numeral. Apart from using the period in a sentence, commas are used very frequently. Sadly, most students (and adults) either forget to use them or misplace them within the sentence.

> My favorite flowers, which are sunflowers, are sitting in a vase in my bedroom.
>
> When in doubt, make sure you study in case there is a pop quiz in class today.
>
> Can you check if the turkey, potatoes, and green beans are fully cooked?

There are some rules to remember when using commas correctly in sentences. Although they may seem simple and that you know all of them, it's always good to have a quick review over them.

Rule 1: The Comma in a Series

Whether it's a list of items or long description, commas are needed to differentiate between each separate item.

> I need to buy some eggs, milk, flour, and butter from the store if you want me to make my famous cookies.
>
> I know that Julian, Curtis, and Karl have signed up for the Mr. Muscle Man pageant.
>
> My favorite comedians include Robin Williams, Steven Martin, and the Three Stooges.

An *oxford comma* is the optional comma before the "and" in a series. Some journalistic writing styles expect the comma to be dropped, but other writing styles, such as critical essays, allow the extra comma to be used before "and".

Rule 2: Commas with Two or More Adjectives

When two or more adjectives are used to describe a noun, commas are used to show distinction between each word. Some examples are below:

My older brother bought the shiniest, fastest, and greatest new car yesterday!

My baby cousin, Stella, has two beautiful, blue eyes and chubby, fat cheeks.

Other than a quick rainstorm, our day out on the lake was fun, exhilarating, and memorable.

Rule 3: Use a comma in every a compound sentence.

Every compound sentence needs a comma before *and, but, and or*. Using a comma helps separate each thought or idea in each individual sentence.

I haven't bought my tickets for the show yet, but Pamela and Helen have.

Donny plans on backpacking in Europe, and Cindy is going to Asia in the summer.

Avery is either related to George Washington, or she is related to a famous writer in Britain.

The following are exercises that will help you use commas better. Simply insert commas correctly into each compound sentence.

EXERCISE D: Commas in Compound Sentence

D.1 The lake isn't frozen enough for us to ice skate on but we can go sledding down the hill instead.

D.2 I took cold medicine this morning and I plan on taking more before I go to bed tonight.

D.3 Elle either went to the ballet practice this morning or she went yesterday morning before school.

D.4 Take a spoonful of sugar and sprinkle it over the entire batter.

D.5 Dean is the new mascot for the football team and Annie was hired as the new student coordinator.

D.6 You need to sign up for the SAT prep course or you need to start studying on your own.

D.7 I'm excited for June's party because June's dad who just got back from Afghanistan will be there.

D.8 Have you heard U2's new music or have you been finding other new music?

D.9 I'm ready to go to dinner but are Daniel and Raquel ready?

D.10 When it comes to staying active Taylor likes to run but John would rather lift weights.

Rule 4: Use a comma before or after introductory words.

To help separate extra words and phrases from the independent sentence, commas are used to show separation and that the word or clause is an addition to the sentence.

> First, I would like to congratulate your success on getting admitted into this highly competitive program.
>
> Janice still turned in her final research report even though it was considered late, however.
>
> On the other hand, President George Bush is still considered a great president who did so much for this country.

Rule 5: Insert a comma when nonessential words or clauses are used in a sentence.

As stated in the previous rule, commas are inserted before and after words or clauses that aren't a part of the independent clause and sentence. They help the reader understand the sentence better; otherwise, he or she would be very confused about what the sentence is trying to say.

> Mrs. Tao, a black belt and karate expert, demonstrated a few moves in front of the class full of beginners.
>
> Tammy, even though she was late for her recital, received a round of applause for her outstanding performance.
>
> A former Olympic champion, Judd Jameson still visits the first gym that he used to work out at.

The following are exercises that need commas inserted correctly into each sentence. Simply place commas where they are needed. Answers are provided in the back of the book so you can check your work.

EXERCISE E: Commas for Nonessential Words or Clauses

E.1 Convinced that it wasn't a joke Mrs. Curtis filed a complaint against the entire senior class because of their school prank.

E.2 In this case however I believe that Lionel has a right to be mad at you.

E.3 Quail even though you don't understand it is a delicacy in some countries.

E.4 Lastly I believe that I should be accepted into your engineering program because I want to become aerospace engineer and work for NASA.

E.5 Kendall the winner of the spelling bee for four years in a row lost to Mindy this afternoon.

E.6 Daniel Radcliffe known for his role as Harry Potter is now starring in other movies in hopes to stop being associated with his first role.

E.7 Second I would love to thank my mom and dad for supporting during high school.

E.8 Other than being the middle sister Florence has always been overlooked in her family and at school.

E.9 Listen to your parents; otherwise you may make a mistake that you can't take back.

E.10 Donald Trump known for controversial behavior is a great philanthropist who gives back to the community.

Commas are a part of everyday writing, so it's important to understand how to use them properly. Most high school students struggle with throwing commas randomly into sentences, which was something that they probably got away with in elementary school. However, high school (and especially college) is a totally different type of environment. Teachers expect you to understand what a comma is and how to use it. Take your time to review this section ad check your answers to see if you've mastered the comma.

A *question mark* (?) is a punctuation mark that indicates a question. Question marks are used occasionally, and more than likely you know how to properly use them.

> What are we going to eat for dinner tonight?
>
> Can you tell me where the nearest gas station is located?
>
> Despite the disappointment of losing, do you still want to go to a restaurant and eat something?

Quotation marks (" ") either mark the beginning and end of a title or quoted passage or to indicate that a word or phrase is regarded as slang or jargon or is being discussed rather than used within the sentence. There are many different uses for quotation marks, such as:

- Quotations (whether quoting a part of another written document or something another person has said)

> Greg Lyon's review of the new book said it was "uplifting, funny, and inspiring".
>
> "Amazing grace, how sweet the sound" are some of the most famous lyrics ever written and sung.
>
> My teacher said that my paper was "more than satisfactory" and only gave me a B+.

- An unusual word used

  My mother asked me what "my homies" meant, and I burst out loud with laughter.

  My boss said that the "newbies" have to clean up the office before they leave every day.

  Whether or not you use it on a regular basis, "what's up dawg" is not a cool saying anymore.

- A title of a poem, article or book

  "Wuthering Heights" is considered one of the most well written books of the English language.

  In his poem, "The Good Morrow", John Donne writes about an awakening love between a young couple.

  Can you explain to me the meaning and synopsis of "The Iliad"?

The following are exercises that need quotation marks inserted correctly. Simply write quotation marks around the word(s) that require them.

EXERCISE F: Quotation Marks

F.1   The food reviewer of the new restaurant located in lower downtown said that the specialty dishes are superb and fresh.

F.2   Have you ever read Dickens' A Christmas Carol, Our Mutual Friend, or Oliver Twist?

F.3   Please explain to grandma what LOL means.

F.4   My favorite plays by Shakespeare are Hamlet, Othello, Romeo and Juliet, and The Tempest.

F.5   Johnny, why do your guy friends call you bro?

F.6   According to the article in Woodfield Daily, the new park that just opened up is safe for kids, fun for the whole family, and a great place for a cookout.

F.7   In his poem Bright Star, John Keats writes about his love for a girl named Fanny.

F.8   God Bless American isn't sung as much nowadays at baseball games or other sporting events.

F.9   Do you understand what's going on in The Bell Jar by Sylvia Plath?

F.10   Although you don't understand its meaning, calling someone a bro is a term of endearment.

Typically, you don't use quotations in everyday writing, but it's very important to understand when they are needed. For example, when you take the AP English, SAT or ACT tests, some prompts may require you to discuss a novel or poem in the essay. Using quotation marks helps identify the name of the novel or poem that is discussed within the essay. If you're still having trouble with using quotation marks, there are additional links in the back of the book that will help you understand it better.

A *hyphen* is (-) is a punctuation mark that used to join words to indicate that they have a combined meaning or that they are linked in the grammar of a sentence, to indicate the division of a word at the end of a line, or to indicate a missing or implied element.

This is one type of punctuation that some high school students struggle with using correctly. When using a compound adjective, usually a hyphen is needed. However, if the compound adjective uses an adverb, then a hyphen is not used. Below are some examples of the hyphen's different uses.

> My 2-year-old niece always has a smile on her face whenever I see her.
>
> The red-orange blouse will look really cute for date night!
>
> Remember, every –ed word is in the past tense, not the present tense.
>
> Please don't interrupt me again. What I was saying was—

The following are exercises that will help you learn how to use hyphens better. Simply insert the hyphen where it needs to be. Answers are included in the back of the book.

EXERCISE G: Hyphens

G.1 Hey! Stop that truck

G.2 Can you please help me find my blue green scarf to wear to dinner tonight?

G.3 My 11 year old brother can do the neatest tricks.

G.4 Wait, I was just about to

G.5 Please pick out your favorite clear coated primer paint.

G.6 When you use *ing*, it depicts that the word is showing present action.

G.7 Other than the other shirt I picked out, I think the grayish white one looks best on you.

G.8 Gerald's hand me down shirts and pant look too big on his frame.

G.9 Until school is over, you need to keep up with day to day homework assignments.

G.10 I have no clue where this road is

Hyphens are a necessary evil in the English language, so it's important to understand their function. Think of it this way—hyphens either help connect words to form a new meaning or show separation within a text. They're essentially helping the reader understand the text better.

An ***ellipsis*** (…) is a set of dots that depicts an omission from speech or writing. These are typically used in dialogue or when a train of thought trails off. Most likely, ellipsis won't be used in your writing very often because they generally show up in novels, plays, or other pieces of dialogue.

> On second thought, maybe I shouldn't have cut my hair so short…
>
> Please…come back and marry me after this war is over…
>
> I'm sorry; I don't understand where you're going with that train of thought…

Even though ellipsis are pretty easy to understand, take a moment to review the material so you can master the ellipses and identify it in plays or novels. You can even impress your teacher with the knowledge of knowing what an ellipses is.

An ***apostrophe*** (') is a punctuation mark that shows either possession or the absence of letters or numbers. Apostrophes are very important to understand and use properly. Not only do they help show possession, but apostrophes also help create contractions.

> The dog's left paw
>
> Olivia's new leather purse
>
> A chair's old cushion

There are a few rules to follow in regards to apostrophes, such as using them correctly to show single and plural possession and contractions.

Rule 1: Use an apostrophe to show singular possession.

I was at Kiki's house the other day watching the football game.

Can you tell that my shirt's color has faded?

Please help me carry this bin to the gym's storage room.

Rule 2: Use an apostrophe to show plural possession.

Why can't we have a car just like the Joneses' car?

Guys' night is filled with video games, pizza, and talking smack.

The camels' trough wasn't filled with water the last time I checked.

Rule 3: Use an apostrophe to show a contraction.

I just can't belleve you decided to cram last minute for our midterm.

Doesn't Paula's mom run the vintage store in downtown?

The twins weren't ready for their music lesson, so they had to skip it.

The following are exercises that require you to place the apostrophe correctly in the sentences. Answers are provided in the back of the book for reference. Make sure you take your time and go through each exercise thoroughly.

EXERCISE H: Apostrophe

H.1   Please dont throw my old shoes away.

H.2   Beckys twin sister attends Penn University.

H.3   The cats food bowl was spilt everywhere when I got home. (hint: plural)

H.4   Ashlynns diary is full of stupid stuff about boys and drama with girls.

H.5   Honey, have you seen Professor Judy and Jims research report around here?

H.6   Wont you consider studying a little harder for geography in the future?

H.7   Plenty of peoples attention are distracted by social media lately. Its bad.

H.8   Underneath the windowsill, youll find our mothers new pet.

H.9   Cant you study without the rest of your study group?

H.10 I couldnt be that nice to my sibling, if youd ask me.

Apostrophes are very important and, after review, are very easy to understand. After practicing the above exercises, you should be able to master the apostrophe now. If you are still having trouble, additional links are provided in the end of this guide.

A *slash* (/) is a punctuation mark that is inserted in between alternatives, fractions, ratios, or between separate elements of a text. Typically, slashes aren't used in everyday writing.

> I think we need ⅔ cup of butter, ¼ cup of sugar, and ½ cup of water.
>
> His/her bathrooms are located in the far right of the restaurant.
>
> Please pick whether you want chicken/beef/tofu tacos.

It's best to understand slashes and how to use them correctly. Make sure to use them only when they are needed.

Brackets [ ] are a pair of marks used to enclose words to separate them from the text. Once again, brackets aren't used in everyday writing, but knowing how to use them will come in handy for technical papers, such as scientific reports or literary essays.

> After collecting data [courtesy of the University of Michigan], we finally solve the problem.
>
> Healthcliff [a character in "Wuthering Heights"] is seen as having a voracious, demonic presence.
>
> After reviewing this poem [with deconstructionism criticisms], I discovered more hidden themes in it.

Usually, brackets should only be used sparingly; if used too much, then they look jarring in sentences and break up the flow. That why it's best to use brackets in either critical or scientific essays.

A *dash* is a punctuation mark that depicts a pause, interjection, or break in sense, or to represent omitted letters or words. Dashes are used very often in poetry and dialogue in plays or novels, but can appear elsewhere in writing.

I don't even know where to begin now—

But—I'm not sure if Peggy can be in the play this year.

Clara Wright—you know, the girl with fiery red hair and green eyes— won the race.

The following are exercises that will help you learn how to use slashes, brackets, and dashes correctly. Circle *slash, bracket,* or *dash* at the end of the sentence. Determine which punctuation mark is needed.

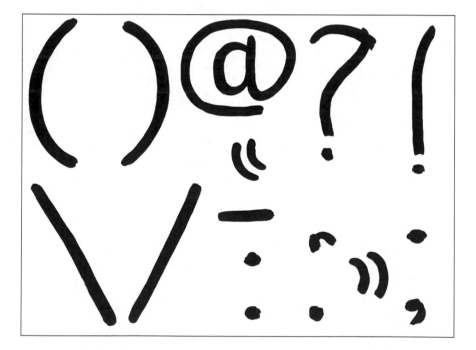

EXERCISE I: Slash, Bracket, or Dash

I.1   Do you want pizza a burger a steak? (slash, bracket, or dash)

I.2   As discovered in *The Age of Innocence* written by Edith Wharton, frivolity and societal judgment have always been major themes in novels. (slash, bracket, or dash)

I.3   The Pythagorean theorem established by Pythagoras has proven true through centuries and centuries. (slash, bracket, or dash)

I.4   Oh, where did I put my keys and hat (slash, bracket, or dash)

I.5   Are these shoes considered his her? (slash, bracket, or dash)

I.6   Other than dyeing my hair, I didn't plan on rebelling against my parents (slash, bracket, or dash)

I.7   As I understand now, there is only one his her bathroom in this store. (slash, bracket, or dash)

I.8   Harvard University established by the greatest educators in America is still one of the top universities in the country. (slash, bracket, or dash)

I.9   You need to believe me. I saw a ghost over there (slash, bracket, or dash)

I.10   Do you want to buy a car truck for your next car of choice? (slash, bracket, or dash)

Hopefully this section didn't overwhelm you too much. Punctuation can be dry to learn, but it's very important to understand how to use them correctly. Essentially, punctuation marks make or break a sentence. They diffuse confusion and make it easy for readers to understand the sentence. Let's move onto the next: common phrasal verbs.

Common Phrasal Verbs

Common phrasal verbs are verbs and other words that are paired and commonly used together. There are three different types of common phrasal verbs: separable phrasal verbs, inseparable (transitive) phrasal verbs, three-word (transitive) phrasal verbs, and intransitive phrasal verbs.

Separable phrasal verbs are phrasal verbs when an object sometimes comes after or may separate the two parts:

Throw away the old groceries.

Throw the old groceries **away**.

Some separate phrasal verbs include the following:

- To Blow Up
- To Bring Up
- To Call Off
- To Do Over
- To Fill Out
- To Fill Up
- To Find Out
- To Give Away
- To Give Back
- To Hand In
- To Hang Up
- To Hold Up
- To Leave Out
- To Look Over
- To Look Up
- To Make Up
- To Make Out
- To Pick Out
- To Pick Up
- To Point Out
- To Put Away
- To Put Off
- To Put On
- To Put Out
- To Read Over
- To Set Up
- To Take Down
- To Take Off
- To Talk Over
- To Throw Away
- To Try On
- To Try Out
- To Turn Down
- To Turn Off
- To Turn On
- To Use Up

Take your time to understand the different types of verb phrases. Understanding them will help you write stronger sentences and be a better writer overall.

> Please don't **use up** all the gasoline in the car.
>
> Please don't **use** all the gasoline in the car **up**.
>
> I don't have enough time to **make** all my homework **up**.
>
> I don't have enough time to **make up** all my homework.

Below are blanks where you write one sentence using the phrasal verbs together or with the phrasal verbs separated. Examples are given in the back of the book.

EXERCISE J: Verb Phrases

J.1 to fill up

J.2 to read over

J.3 to point out

EXERCISE J: Verb Phrases

J.4   to put away

J.5   to talk over

J.6   to hang up

J.7   to set up

J.8   to give back

EXERCISE J: Verb Phrases

J.9 to put off

J.10 to look over

Knowing and understanding what separable phrasal verbs are will put you ahead of the game above your peers. Make sure you go through each exercises slowly in order to master phrasal verbs. Now, onto the next term.

Inseparable (transitive) phrasal verbs are verbs that cannot be separated from the prepositions (or other parts) that accompany it.

> We must **go through** this horrible traffic in order to get to the play on time.
>
> You won't believe it! We just saw a turkey **run across** the road!
>
> Let's **go over** these literary terms again before the final.

Here are a few examples of inseparable phrasal verbs:

- To Call On
- To Go Through
- To Run Across
- To Get over

- To Look After
- To Run Into
- To Wait On
- To Go Over

- To Look Into
- To Take After

Below are blanks for you to create your own sentences using the given inseparable phrasal verbs. Examples are provided in the back of the book.

EXERCISE K: Inseparable Phrasal Verbs
K.1 to take over
K.2 to look into
K.3 to wait on
K.4 to call on
K.5 to go through

EXERCISE K: Inseparable Phrasal Verbs

K.6	to look after
K.7	to run across
K.8	to run into
K.9	to take after
K.10	to go over

Now that you've survived through those two types of phrasal verbs, let's conquer the last two types. Hopefully, you've mastered those and are ready to move on.

Three-Word (transitive) phrasal verbs are composed of three words that make up a phrasal verb. These phrasal verbs are typically used in daily conversation. (And you've probably never noticed that you and your friends use them all the time!)

Aw man, we **ran out of** clean towels and clothes.

We need to **check up on** Chelsea to see if her cold is any better.

How dare you **talk back to** your teacher that way, Andrew!

Here are some examples of three-word phrasal verbs that you probably use very often:

- To Break In On
- To Catch Up With
- To Check Up On
- To Come Up With
- To Cut Down On
- To Drop Out Of
- To Get Along With
- To Get Away With
- To Get Rid Of
- To Get Through With
- To Keep Up With
- To Look Down On
- To Look Out For
- To Look Up To
- To Look In On
- To Put Up With
- To Run Out Of
- To Make Sure Of
- To Talk Back To
- To Think Back On
- To Take Care of

The following are blank sentences where you will create your own sentences with the given three-word phrasal verbs. Examples are given in the back of the book.

EXERCISE L: Three-Word Phrasal Verbs

L.1   break in on

L.2   put up with

L.3   look in on

L.4   keep up with

L.5   to get rid of

EXERCISE L: Three-Word Phrasal Verbs
L.6   to make sure of
L.7   to take care of
L.8   to get along with
L.9   to catch up with
L.10   look out for

You've survived the three types of phrasal verbs. Now there's only one more to go. Let's tackle it.

Intransitive phrasal verbs are phrasal verbs that are not followed by an object.

Hey, are you going to **drop by** soon?

Please **keep away** from my rose bushes!

Sorry, dude, I'm going to go home and **pass out**.

Here are some examples of intransitive phrasal verbs:

- Break Down
- Catch On
- Come Back
- Come In
- Come To
- Come Over
- Drop By
- Eat Out
- Get By
- Get Up
- Go Back
- Go On
- Grow Up
- Keep Away
- Keep On
- Pass Out
- Show Off
- Show up

Below are blank sentences where you will create your own sentences with the given intransitive phrasal verbs. Examples are provided in the back of the book. Take your time so you fully understand how to use the phrase correctly.

EXERCISE M: Intransitive Phrasal Verbs
M.1   show off
M.2   keep on

EXERCISE M: Intransitive Phrasal Verbs
M.3   pass out
M.4   get by
M.5   pass out
M.6   come back
M.7   eat out

EXERCISE M: Intransitive Phrasal Verbs
M.8   catch on
M.9   come to
M.10 come over

Conclusion

After going through rules and exercises of punctuation and common phrasal verbs, you may feel very overwhelmed by everything. Don't stress out—you've got this. Take your time, and do the best that you can. Finally, all the technical, hard stuff is over, and you can move onto forming great sentences.

"All you have to do is write one true sentence.
Write the truest sentence that you know."

- ERNEST HEMINGWAY

CHAPTER 13
Sentence Fragments

One of the most debilitating factors that injure sentences is sentence fragments. Unfortunately, most high school students write them all the time because they don't pay attention to what they are writing and don't review their work. Sentence fragments will look really bad to future employers, teachers, and other adults if you have them in your essays or other written documents.

This chapter will review what sentence fragments are and how to avoid them. It's very important to study each definition, example, and exercises. Take your time as you work through each rule, too.

Now let's start tackling sentence fragments.

The first step to stop writing sentence fragments is to recognize the difference between a fragment and sentence. A *sentence fragment* is contains everything in sentence but a main clause. Main clauses are the most vital piece to making a sentence—well, a sentence. Sentence fragments are startling because they miss that essential portion of the sentence that makes it a complete thought. Here are some (very wrong) examples:

Flew away from the burning tree.

The woman kneeling on the floor near by.

Troubled without hope in sight.

As mentioned before, a sentence is composed of a subject, verb, and complete thought. With one of these parts, you create a sentence fragment.

Subject + verb + complete thought (main clause) = sentence

If you struggle with using sentence fragments, there's good news for you: it's a mistake that's very easy to fix. You can either add a complete thought (main clause) to the fragment or connect the fragment to another clause that is in the body of your paragraph (if you have one).

Sentence fragments are typically an appositive, verb phrase, afterthought, subordinate clause, participle phrase or infinitive phrase. Below are descriptions of each type of sentence fragment. Let's begin with an appositive sentence fragment.

An ***appositive phrase*** sentence fragment starts off with a noun and phrase after it. There is no complete thought at the end of this fragment.

Ginny the girl who loved her pet hedgehog so much.

The otter that swam away so fast from me.

The tennis team that was losing almost every game.

The following are appositive phrases. Complete the sentence fragment by inserting a verb and complete thought. Examples are provided in the back of the book.

EXERCISE A: Appositive Phrase

A.1   Linda the head of the school board

A.2   The owl that slept during the day

A.3   Harry Potter the boy who lived

A.4   Pauline who lived in Alaska for most of her life

A.5   The box that's been on the shelf for so many years

EXERCISE A: Appositive Phrase
A.6 Jenelle the girl with a really good fast pitch
A.7 The fence that only I can jump over
A.8 Diana a Greek goddess
A.9 Lobsters that are caught in Maine
A.10 The water color painting that was in the art museum

Appositive sentence fragments are some of the most commonly used fragments. Make sure you rewrite the sentence fragment and include a main clause at the end of the sentence.

A *subordinate clause sentence fragment* is only composed of a subordinate clause, lacking a subject and verb. This type of fragment is one of the worst mistakes that you can do. Here are some examples:

> Because there was no more food or water.
>
> Underneath the border and trim.
>
> Such as cutting out fatty foods.

In order to fix these fragments, you must insert a subject and verb into the sentence to complete the thought.

> I went to the store to grab some supplies **because there was no more food or water**.
>
> Whitney found some hidden dust particles **underneath the border and trim**.
>
> The best way to lose weight is to eat healthy, **such as cutting out fatty foods**.

Below are subordinate clauses. Complete the sentence fragment by inserting a subject and verb. Examples are provided in the back of the book.

EXERCISE B: Subordinate Clauses
B.1   Even though the wait was almost over

EXERCISE B: Subordinate Clauses

B.2   After everything was thoroughly finished

B.3   Behind the tattered, velvet curtain

B.4   During the beautiful wedding reception in downtown

B.5   Other than being embarrassed by the fall

B.6   Beneath the blankets and covers

EXERCISE B: Subordinate Clauses
B.7   Onto the kitchen door
B.8   Before the quintet ended the performance
B.9   Under the tree where I read books
B.10   Situated between two hills

A ***verb phrase*** sentence fragment is a fragment that is composed of only verbs and their descriptive words. This is also one of the worst mistakes you can make. Here are some examples below:

Checked the amount of time he had left

Roasted the turkey for the entire afternoon

Punished all three children because of their behavior

Below are verb phrases. Complete the sentence fragment by inserting a subject and object. Examples are provided in the back of the book.

EXERCISE C: Verb Phrase Sentence Fragments
C.1   Ate with my entire family and friends
C.2   Kept his journal since middle school
C.3   Bought groceries down the street
C.4   Tried to take her final exam early so she could visit her family
C.5   Juggled five balls at one time

EXERCISE C: Verb Phrase Sentence Fragments

C.6   Can't seem to get all this paint off

C.7   Baked cookies, a cake, and brownies for the bake sale

C.8   Diced up some tomatoes for this recipe

C.9   Knocked on the door to let them know he was there

C.10   Dribbled the basketball like a pro athlete

An *infinitive phrase* sentence fragment lacks a complete thought and subject. People generally speak in these sentence fragments in everyday speech. Here are some examples:

To go to rehearsal practice for the school play

To play hide-and-seek with the younger children

To hold the flowers for the bride at the altar

Below are infinitive phrases. Complete the sentence fragment by inserting a subject and object. Examples are provided in the back of the book.

EXERCISE D: Infinitive Phrase Sentence Fragments
D.1   To arrange the flowers in the prettiest manner
D.2   To write in the most succinct way
D.3   To play guitar as good as my brother

EXERCISE D: Infinitive Phrase Sentence Fragments

D.4   To make goodie bags for the homeless this holiday season

D.5   To hand out prizes to the winners of the convention

D.6   To get gas and start on our journey

D.7   To gather all the leaves into one pile

D.8   To hide from all the grownups in the house

EXERCISE D: Infinitive Phrase Sentence Fragments
D.9   To decorate the house for fall and Christmas
D.10   To nominate the homecoming king and queen for this year

An ***afterthought*** sentence fragment is an added-on thought after a complete sentence was written or said beforehand. Most teenagers text and speak in abbreviated sentence fragments, thus causing them to slip up in essays and other writing assignments. Below are some examples:

Should've been done yesterday

Probably didn't do a great job with it

If only it went this way instead of that

Below are afterthought phrases. Complete the sentence fragment by inserting a subject and object. Examples are provided in the back of the book.

EXERCISE E: Afterthought Sentence Fragments
E.1   Just when I thought that I was done with school for good

EXERCISE E: Afterthought Sentence Fragments

E.2   Could've done much better than I did on that test

E.3   Probably just going to go to sleep now

E.4   Would've gone to the baseball game instead of class

E.5   Instead of staying up until 3 in the morning

E.6   Just need to stop and take a deep breath

EXERCISE E: Afterthought Sentence Fragments
E.7   Wish I had a few A's rather than C's
E.8   Can't believe Katie isn't coming to my graduation party
E.9   Should've ordered my school uniform months ago instead of now
E.10   Tried to maneuver out of detention already

A *participle phrase* sentence fragment is a description of something that lacks a subject and complete thought. Here are some examples:

Running away from the scene as fast as he could

Looking out the window from time to time for the past hour

Carving the piece of wood with his grandfather's knife

Below are participle phrases. Complete the sentence fragment by inserting a subject and object. Examples are provided in the back of the book.

EXERCISE F: Participle Phrase Sentence Fragments
F.1 Pulling the long trailer behind the truck
F.2 Figuring out if I want to go to band practice or not
F.3 Sailing from Florida to Maine this summer after school is out
F.4 Wanting to go skiing in the Alps during Christmas break
F.5 Herding all the sheep into the pen once night falls

EXERCISE F: Participle Phrase Sentence Fragments
F.6 Circling all the wrong answers on my midterm test
F.7 Studying for the SAT and ACT all summer long
F.8 Winning the state championship within the last quarter
F.9 Knitting a couple of hats, scarves, and mittens for my family
F.10 Looking terrified from the amount of homework we were assigned

Conclusion

As easy as it is to speak in sentence fragments, it's not always easy to leave them out in your writing. Hopefully this section helped you understand what sentence fragments are, what each type looks like, and how to correct them. If you can avoid using sentence fragments, then your writing will improve immensely—just like that. Let's now move onto other outside factors that weaken sentence, such as dangling modifiers.

"A word after a word after a word is power."

- MARGARET ATWOOD

CHAPTER 14
Dangling Modifiers

Every writer—whether it's Stephen King or a high school student—struggles with dangling modifiers. Not only do they appear in everyday speech, but they also come up in writing. It's very easy to accidently use them, but with great editing skills you'll be able to identify dangling modifiers and fix them. Work slowly through this section to master dangling modifiers.

Dangling modifiers are words, phrases, or clauses that are incorrectly placed; that is, dangling modifiers are written or spoken errors. Here are some examples:

> Terrified, the haunted bedroom made the girl run to her parents' room.
>
> Panting, the ravaging dog was no longer in sight.
>
> Tired, the dirty mattress looked better than having nothing to sleep on.

Most dangling modifiers are caused by a similar mistake: having no target. A modifier's main job is to modify a target, so when a sentences lacks a target, a dangling modifier is created. Here are a few things to ask yourself when fixing dangling modifier blunders.

1. Is there a dangling modifier in this sentence?

2. Do I need to rearrange this sentence to fix the mistake?

3. If so, does the modifier need a target or purpose?

4. Do I need to add anything else to the sentence to make it correct?

To tackle the first question, examine the sentence closely.

> Hungry, she saw that the restaurant was closed for the night.

Hungry is a dangling modifier, so this sentence needs to be fixed.

To answer the second question, think about how you need to change the sentence to eliminate the dangling modifier.

Yes, the sentence needs to be arranged differently.

Next, identify whether the dangling modifier needs an object or another purpose.

> Hungry, she saw that the restaurant was closed for the night.

In this particular situation, the adjective *Hungry* needs an object. Clearly, the adjective is linked to the female in the sentence, so now you have your target chosen.

Let's rearrange this sentence now.

> She, feeling hungry, saw that the restaurant was closed for the night.

To answer the last question, examine the sentence again. As you can see, the sentence is now fixed and doesn't need any more changes. Now it's your turn.

Below are exercises that will help you with learning how to recognize dangling modifiers and fix them during revisions. Circle the dangling modifier in the sentence then rewrite the sentence.

EXERCISE A: Dangling Modifiers
A.1 Crying, the little girl ran over to her mom for comfort.
A.2 The teacher shook her head at the rambunctious classroom, dismayed.
A.3 Lying, the skeptical lawyer walked briskly away from his client.
A.4 Candace, the last woman to leave the room, hurried home, tired.

EXERCISE A: Dangling Modifiers

A.5   Manny faked a pass and won the game with a great run into the end zone, elated.

A.6   Stubborn, neither boy owned up to his mistake, so they stayed in time out.

A.7   Ewan wrote his girlfriend a love letter, head over heels.

A.8   Dismayed, Lionel should still apologize even if he was in the right.

A.9   Tragic, the old woman's death was a hard blow to everyone in the community.

EXERCISE A: Dangling Modifiers

A.10 Gwen, the newest dancer on the team, beamed brightly on the stage, excited.

Dangling modifiers aren't as difficult to correct as most people think. Because they are used in everyday language, they easily get mixed up in formal, written language. But once you become a pro at detecting them in your work, then you'll start to eliminate them more, which will improve your writing.

Now, let's tackle gerunds, participles and idioms.

"Cut out all these exclamation points. An exclamation point is like laughing at your own joke."

- F. SCOTT FITZGERALD

CHAPTER 15

Gerunds, Participles, and Idioms

This section may confuse you. You probably have never heard of a gerund before (or just haven't heard that term in a very long time). Gerunds, participles and idioms are technical terms that terrify most students and greatly deter them from mastering what they are and how and when to use them.

Have no fear—they aren't as scary as they appear. Once you've gone through this chapter and learned what they are, you will become a master of these technical terms and impress your friends (and definitely your teacher!).

First off, let's begin with gerunds.

A **gerund** is a form that is derived from a verb but functions as a noun, such as *do you mind me **taping** this interview?*

So, a gerund is just a fancy term for something that you use in everyday speech. When you add *–ing* to the end of a verb, the verb turns into a gerund. Here are some examples.

Reading is a great pastime that encourages brain activity and an engaged imagination.

I know I just started, but **rowing** is my favorite sport to participate in.

My favorite stress-relieving activities are **knitting** and **crocheting**.

You may wonder why you need to understand what a gerund is, but the answer is quite simple. If you want to be a true master of grammar and a prolific writer, then you must know all the fancy terms and grammar rules. Although a gerund is only a verb-turned-noun, it's still good to understand this term.

Let's practice finding gerunds in sentences.

The following are a few exercises that will help you understand gerunds more. Circle the gerund in the sentence. Answers are provided in the back of the book.

EXERCISE A: Gerund

A.1 Did you take Rachel to her first swimming lessons last week?

A.2 Other than that, I'd say that cooking is my strongest passion outside of panning for gold.

A.3 Frederick and Mindy both enjoy hunting for deer and turkeys this time of year.

A.4 Lydia, my first cousin, is an all-state winner in running and jumping hurdles.

A.5 While you were away, I started fencing lessons again with Mr. Williams.

A.6 I never knew that you enjoyed writing so much, Jessica!

A.7 Today is a brilliant day to go hiking in the woods.

A.8 Paulina told Michael that she used to win biking competitions years ago.

A.9 Whenever I'm home for the summer, I enjoy fishing in nearby streams.

A.10 On top of that, I've been told that I'm a quick finisher when it comes to testing.

Hopefully after those exercises, you'll understand gerunds better. Knowing the correct definition and terminology of grammar terms is vital to becoming a great writer. And you're one step closer to becoming one of the greats! Now let's move on to participles.

A *participle* is a word formed from a verb and is used as an adjective or a noun. Participles are also used to make compound verb forms. There are three functions, too: participles can form multi-part verbs, act as an adjective or function as a noun.

Participles appear in sentences much more than you might think. From daily conversations to novels, they compose most of our everyday language. Understanding what they are and what purpose they function is very important. This section will take you through some examples and also make you practice identifying them as well.

Here are some examples of participles as multi-part verbs:

> Jacob **has been eating** all the strawberries, so I don't have enough to make strawberry cobbler.
>
> I **was wondering** if you could stop by the store this afternoon for your father.
>
> You **should have known** better than to pick vegetables from Mrs. Kit's garden.

Here are some examples of participles as adjectives:

> The **broken** branch dangled in the air above my head.
>
> Can you fix this **mangled** necklace? I can't seem to do it.
>
> The **crouching** kitten eyed the bowl of milk on the counter this morning.

And here are examples of participles as nouns:

> Instead of **criticizing** her work, the teacher gave the student tips on how to improve it.
>
> Can you stop **watching** TV and help me cook this dinner?
>
> I'd rather stay here and feel better than be **sneezing** all day around other people.

Understanding what participles are may confuse you, but with practice, you'll be able to pick them out easily in sentences. Try to identify a participle the next time you have a conversation with your friend. You may be surprised at how many participles pop up in your everyday jargon.

The following are examples of participles in multi-part verbs, as adjectives or as nouns. Circle the correct word(s). As an extra bonus, try to identify which particles are multi-part verbs, adjectives or nouns. Answers are provided in the back of the book.

EXERCISE B: Participle

B.1 No wonder you're not hungry; you've been eating all day long!

B.2 Can you quiet this crying baby? She doesn't seem to like me holding her.

B.3 Instead of diving for lobsters, can we go snorkeling in the Keys this weekend?

B.4 Penelope is my sleeping cat's name.

B.5 The Jacksonville Jaguars have not been playing well this football season.

B.6 Other than last week, the deafening noise hasn't occurred again.

B.7 Can you make sure Matilda doesn't miss school again?

B.8 Sydney, the school nurse, hasn't made Lily go back to see her next week.

B.9 Before you head to town next, make sure the crinkling flowers get watered.

B.10 Little did you know that I was about to head to the farmers market to buy vegetables.

Once mastered, participles are very easy to understand and do pepper sentences with variations. Although you may think you can slide by without mastering this grammatical term, but think again. It's important to learn the essential building blocks that foster great writing. Now let's move onto our last term—idioms.

An *idiom* is a group of words established by usage as having a meaning not deductible from those of the individual words. In other words, a form of expression that is understood in a culture or by a specific group of people. Idioms appear in everyday conversation, whether you notice them or not. They also pepper pop culture on TV and the Internet.

As for how idioms originated, no one is really sure. There are idioms that form over time in different eras and also different countries. For instance, idioms in America would probably confuse anybody from a different country. The same goes for British idioms and so on. Despite how they came about, idioms have stuck around and are jargon that's used in daily conversation.

As a slight warning, you must be careful how to use idioms. In some academic scenarios, idioms are frowned upon as 'poor writing' and sound too cliché for good use. However, in other scenarios, idioms are perfectly okay to use. When you're trying to explain something in a conversation, idioms can be a useful and quick way to convey what you mean.

Here are some examples of idioms:

> That high-definition TV is going to cost you **an arm and a leg**.
> I'm going to take Buddy for a run to **kill two birds with one stone**.
> I already told you want days I'm available, so **the ball is in your court**.

After reading those examples, you've probably heard and seen those idioms elsewhere. Idioms are typically pretty easy to understand and very easy to identify in a sentence. It's important that you understand the correct definition for this term, so you can understand their purpose better.

Let's do two exercises for this section. The first exercise will consist of identifying the idiom in the sentence by circling it, and the second exercise will have you create your own sentences with given idioms. Let's get started, shall we?

Below are exercises that ask you to identify the idiom in the sentence. Circle or highlight the idiom. Answers are provided in the back of the book.

EXERCISE C: Idiom

C.1 I told George to hurry up; he's always a day late and a dollar short.

C.2 Tracy did warn Kim; she bit off more than she could chew.

C.3 Cry me a river, Sam. I don't believe that you're sorry.

C.4 Well, folks, Elvis has left the building.

C.5 I don't think I can go to work today; I'm feeling under the weather.

C.6 Good luck, Jim! Break a leg out there on the stage!

C.7 I'm sorry; I made a hasty decision in the heat of the moment.

C.8 To make a long story short, I finally told him how I felt about the situation.

C.9 I hope Mrs. McPhee got a taste of her own medicine!

C.10 Well, you're guess is as good as mine, Mr. Sanders.

The following are exercises that ask you to create your own sentences with given idioms. Feel free to be as creative as you want. Examples are provided in the back of the book for guidance.

EXERCISE D: Create Your Own Sentences with Given Idioms

D.1   Wouldn't be caught dead

D.2   Take with a grain of salt

D.3   Speak of the devil

D.4   See eye to eye

D.5   Piece of Cake

EXERCISE D: Create Your Own Sentences with Given Idioms
D.6   See through rose-colored glasses
D.7   Method to my madness
D.8   Can't teach an old dog new tricks
D.9   Keep something at bay
D.10   It takes two to tango

After going through each example and exercise, you probably feel more confident about understanding idioms and how and when to use them. Although you should avoid using them while writing papers in high school, college and so on, idioms are a part of our everyday language, so using them in relaxed conversation is perfectly acceptable. Idioms are just one of the grammatical tools that make our language and how we communicate the way it is today.

Hopefully you understand gerunds, participles and idioms more than you did before. (And if you knew these grammatical terms already, then excellent job!) Relearning terms and going through every exercise isn't always the easiest task to do, but your writing skills will improve because of it, guaranteed.

The last chapters in section two drift away from pesky terms and are geared toward tuning your language in order to become a prolific writer. These next chapters are extremely vital to improving not only your sentences, but your overall writing style. Take your time going through each chapter, and don't hesitate to double-check your answers in the back of the book.

With that said, let's now move on a very important chapter: diction and word choice.

> "Any word you have to hunt for in a thesaurus is the wrong word. There are no exceptions to this rule."
>
> **- STEPHEN KING**

CHAPTER 16
Diction/Word Choice

Diction is the backbone of writing. Every sentence you craft depends on which diction you use. From writing emails to tackling a thesis, diction play a part in what you say and how you say it. If done right, diction can take your writing to a whole new level with studying and practice. In other words, diction makes or breaks your entire writing style.

In today's society, diction has been put on the back burner for a couple of reasons (See how I used an idiom in that sentence?) Due to the Internet and texting on cellphones, teenagers typically shorten their words in conversation and writing and throw all grammar rules out the window. Language changes with every new generation, and so teenagers have learned to speak in a totally new way.

However, when it comes to excelling in the academic world, diction and grammar rules are vital. Whether you are writing a personal essay or lengthy research paper, diction is key to getting into your dream college or earning in an A in a class. As you practice your diction in this chapter, try to practice it in speech, writing and, yes, even texting. This challenge is hard, but will pay off in the end.

In this book, we've dedicated an entire chapter on this topic because it's very important for you to master it. This chapter will be a little more in-depth than others, so you can grasp this topic and become a quick master of it. If you're ready, let's get started.

Diction is the choice and use of words and phrases in speech and writing; in other words, diction is about the way you convey something in writing. With that said, diction is very important to break down for you to comprehend it better.

This chapter will guide you how to determine which grammar, words and phrase are best to use. Hopefully, this section will turn your writing upside— and for the better. These next sections will help you tighten up your language and allow you to create beautiful sentences easily. So let's dive in.

There are two rules for implementing diction into your writing. The first rule is that a word has to be right and accurate when used in a sentence or context in general. The second rule is that a word should be appropriate in the context its in. You may be confused by these rules and definitions, but we'll break it down more for you.

Diction helps separate what's good from the bad when it comes to writing. There are many ways to write a thought or idea down, and some ways are better written than others. That's what this section is for. Let's discover how to write the best sentences with ease.

Here are some examples below:

Will you politely accompany me to the benefit concert and dinner tonight?

Are you going with me to the benefit concert and dinner tonight?

Ain't you going to this event thing with me later?

This example is slightly exaggerated, but with purpose. Diction plays a vital part in how we not only convey our thoughts but also how others comprehend what you are saying. Take a look at the first sentence, and picture the speaker in your mind. Does an image of a British individual pop into your mind? Then move on to the second sentence: what speaker do you envision there? You most likely thought of a typical adult. Now imagine the speaker of the last sentence. Did a southern person pop into your mind?

Now you can see how much diction influences what we say and how we say it. Especially when it comes to writing, diction controls how people comprehend every sentence you write. Let's break down the different types of diction, so you can understand when and where you should use certain types of diction.

There are three types of diction: formal, informal and slang (or also known as colloquialism). These will be explained in more in-depth detail in the rest of this chapter, followed by plenty of examples and exercises for you to practice with.

Formal diction is the type of diction you should use in academic settings and usually when you write. Nowadays, formal diction is barely heard in everyday conversation and usually seen in classic literature. Although formal diction may sound strange to your ear when you hear it, it's technically the correct way to speak.

Here are some examples below:

Would you do me the honor of escorting me on this last dance?

I told Diane that I would be delighted to be her maid of honor.

Little did I know, Joseph was already at the restaurant, ready to propose to me.

The only way you will be able to use formal diction on a regular basis is by reading and through tons of practice. One of the best ways you can improve your diction and vocabulary is through reading the great classics. Here is a list of some of the best classics that are full of great diction:

- *Pride and Prejudice* by Jane Austen
- *Frankenstein* by Mary Shelley
- *The Great Gatsby* by F. Scott Fitzgerald
- *Wuthering Heights* by Emily Brontë
- *Moby Dick* by Herman Melville
- *The Iliad* by Homer
- *Great Expectations* by Charles Dickens
- *The Count of Monte Cristo* by Alexandre Dumas
- *The Scarlet Letter* by Nathaniel Hawthorne
- *The Picture of Dorian Gray* by Oscar Wilde

There are hundreds of other books that will improve your writing besides the ones listed here. Once you pick a book to read, study the language and ask yourself why you enjoy certain sentences more than others. This will help you discover why formal diction flows better and why you should use it in your writing, too.

In this section, we will go through two different types of exercises. The first exercise will ask you to circle "yes" or "no" if the sentence is formal or not. The second one will ask you to rewrite the sentence using formal diction. So let's begin.

Below are exercises that ask you to rewrite the sentence. Take your time writing these sentences, and be as creative as you wish. Examples are provided in the back of the book.

EXERCISE A: Formal Diction Sentence
A.1   Kyle, why'd ya do that for to Kelsey's bike?
A.2   Oh my gosh, can you believe Stacie?
A.3   Like, Harry Potter is my favorite book series of all time.
A.4   Can you chill for a second?
A.5   Wow, my mother is the bomb!

EXERCISE A: Formal Diction Sentence
A.6   After I get out from work, let's chill.
A.7   Ain't that the greatest!
A.8   Cool it, Joshua!
A.9   William and Jake are just so hot, right guys?
A.10   Let me grab my stuff before we hit the road.

The following are exercises that ask you to circle "yes" or "no" if the sentence is written in formal diction or not. Answers are provided in the back of the book.

EXERCISE B: Formal Diction

B.1   Please tell me you have heard of The Beatles! (Yes/No)

B.2   Growing up in Alabama, I ain't never had to wear any shoes. (Yes/No)

B.3   Not only did I finish first, but I also set my personal record! (Yes/No)

B.4   I never not finish my meal whenever we go to Rinaldi's Pizzeria and Kitchen! (Yes/No)

B.5   Just because you're different doesn't mean you're not as good as everyone else. (Yes/No)

B.6   On my way home, I swerved out of the road to avoid hitting a duck. (Yes/No)

B.7   Ava, my niece, is, like, the cutest button ever! (Yes/No)

B.8   Despite my injury, I shot a few hoops on the basketball court yesterday. (Yes/No)

B.9   No one never said that about you, Manuel. (Yes/No)

B.10 All your talking is driving me crazy! (Yes/No)

After going through each exercise, hopefully you understand what formal diction looks like and why it's important. Now let's move on to informal diction.

Informal diction is the type of diction you typically use when you talk or write to your friends or family. Typically, informal diction is okay to use in conversation and certain types of writing. Void of grammatical errors, this type of diction constitutes everyday language. Because nobody uses formal diction all the time, informal diction has taken its place.

Here are some examples:

> Natalie, I love what you did with your hair this afternoon!
>
> Knowing that she's just 11, Lydia played the piano without flaw and with ease.
>
> Yes! The Ravens won the entire series last night, and I'm so excited!

After viewing these examples, you can see that informal diction is just a fancy term for typical, everyday language. However, it's good to understand (and relearn) that this term. Just for practice, below are two exercises that will help you perfect your diction.

Below are exercises that ask you to write your own sentences. Feel free to be as creative as you want. Examples are provided in the back of the book.

EXERCISE C: Informal Diction Sentence
C.1   oak tree, swing, Oliver
C.2   Regina, quill, writing
C.3   lions, sleeping, shade
C.4   Unlike, arrows, target
C.5   Ghana, children, missions

EXERCISE C: Informal Diction Sentence
C.6 Warren, Regina, eating
C.7 Mama bear, cubs, sleep
C.8 Yo-yo, Jack, play
C.9 Quickly, Harold, runs
C.10 Squirrel, nuts, tree

The following are exercises that ask you to circle "yes" or "no" if the sentence is considered informal or not. Answers are provided in the back of the book.

EXERCISE D: Informal Diction

D.1 Can you please take Isaac to the airport on Tuesday morning? (Yes/No)

D.2 I'm excited to go whitewater rafting and kayaking this summer! (Yes/No)

D.3 After all, you ain't quite like the rest of the gang here! (Yes/No)

D.4 Hope ya'll get here before we start the ceremony! (Yes/No)

D.5 After a few guitar lessons, I'll turn into a rock star in no time! (Yes/No)

D.6 Better get a move on it, I don't want to keep my parents waiting. (Yes/No)

D.7 I never not make it to the festival every year! (Yes/No)

D.8 Quick! Help me take Johnny to the hospital to mend his broken hand. (Yes/No)

D.9 Layer the cake with my made-from-scratch, delicious icing. (Yes/No)

D.10 Take only as much as you can eat, William. (Yes/No)

After working through each exercise, you should be able to determine which sentences have great diction or not. As for the last type of diction, pay attention to when and where you should use it. Remember, formal diction is always best, but there are some scenarios where you can get away with informal and slang diction.

Slang (also known as colloquialism) is the type of diction that people use when they disregard grammar rules and shorten words and phrases. Slang typically occurs in different cultures, such as the phrase *ya'll* is often said in southern states in the U.S. It's alright to use slang in some settings (like talking with friends or close family members), but not when it comes to writing. It's frowned upon and will dock you points in school.

In today's society, slang has become a huge part of our culture. From shortened words to run-on sentences, slang has disrupted the formality of language today. It's important to detect what is and isn't slang in this section in order to improve your writing style.

Here are some examples:

ya'll

LOL (laugh out loud)

dude

dope

LMK (let me know)

Bae

Basic

I can't even

You've probably seen this phrases and words mentioned in pop culture on the Internet, social media and TV. After humorous as these phrases are, they should never appear in your writing, especially when applying to college or writing an essay at school.

When practicing not to use slang, it's best to double-check how you speak on a day-to-day basis and make sure that it doesn't appear in your writing. Let's do some exercises that will help you learn how to identify slang and how to re-write sentences that have a few slang words in it. Let's begin.

Below are sentences that require you to rewrite the sentence. Answers are provided in the back of the book.

EXERCISE E: Slang (also known as colloquialism)
E.1   IDK, let me check my planner and see if I have next Friday off.
E.2   Wow, that next CD release from Beyonce is dope!
E.3   Other than that, the new girl in our chemistry class seems basic.
E.4   Did you see Roy snort milk out of his nose? I can't even.

EXERCISE E: Slang (also known as colloquialism)
E.5   Unlike Patrick, this new dude over here is a pretty good waiter.
E.6   Please LMK if you'll be able to make it to Easter dinner next week.
E.7   Always rely on my bae to cheer me up after a bad day.
E.8   I need to go to bed now. TTYL!
E.9   TBH, I prefer wearing jeans to work rather than dresses and dress pants.

EXERCISE E: Slang (also known as colloquialism)

E.10   Man, how am I supposed the pass this class with my D average?

After going through these exercises, you should know that slang isn't the best word choice to use, especially when writing. The more you pay attention to what you're saying and how you say it, the better your writing will improve.

Conclusion

After reading every example and exercise in this chapter, you now understand that diction plays a huge role in your writing. Remember to be aware of how you write and to always eliminate any slang words that shouldn't be there. Now let's move on to another very important chapter—active and passive voice.

"Your intuition knows what to write, so get out of the way."

- **RAY BRADBURY**

CHAPTER 17
Active and Passive Voice

As mentioned at the end of the previous chapter, this chapter is very important to work through slowly and thoroughly. Knowing the difference between active and passive voice not only trips up most high school students, but also college students and even adults. When talking in conversation, most people don't focus on using correct grammar (let alone voice), so when it comes to writing, that makes it all the more difficult to write well. But after working through this chapter, you'll be able to improve it in no time.

In this chapter, you will relearn the correct definitions of active voice and passive voice, view examples of both and practice correcting passive voice. In some scenarios, using passive voice is okay (such as literature), but active voice is always the correct way to write when it comes to essays and so on.

Before we dive into discussing active and passive voice, it's important to note that voice is a vital portion of writing. Without voice, your writing is essentially meaningless. In most writing, you typically don't think about the tone and voice you use; but if you start examining how you write, then you'll begin to notice that there's voice used in every type of writing.

Voice is the tone you use in writing; voice dictates how the reader interprets a text. For instance, there are all different types of voices that you encounter every day. As an example, when you read *The Onion*, the tone is usually sarcastic or humorous. When you read any articles on NPR or BBC, the tone is usually serious, informative and formal. As you can see, voice is very important in order to convey your writing's meaning.

As you work through this chapter, pay attention to the types of voice you come across in your daily reading. Is the tone sarcastic, formal, informal, vernacular or informative? Challenge yourself to identify as many different tones as you possibly can. Watching TV can also help you do this, too. But the best way to identify voice is through reading novels, online articles and any type of print.

The more you study what voice is and how you can use it to better your writing, the better your voice will naturally come out in your writing. As stated before, your voice in writing will improve with practice and reading various materials. If you stick with it, then you'll see results fairly quickly. After briefly going over what voice is, let's now move onto active and passive voice.

Passive voice is when the subject is being acted upon in a sentence; in other words, the subject is not doing the action but rather the object. People generally speak in passive voice in daily conversation, which transfers to their writing, unfortunately. As you might have already discovered, English teachers try to break students from writing in passive voice because it isn't the most effective way to write. (Active voice is considered the best and correct way to write.)

Here are some examples below:

> The ball was thrown from the 5-year-old boy in the stands.
>
> Easter eggs were hidden by the mother during her children's Easter egg hunt.
>
> Connie's children were taught to never run out in the road from their grandmother.

As you can see, these sentences may appear to be correct because you've either heard or seen sentences that are similar to these examples. However, these sentences are passive voice. If you write in this style, then let's start breaking this terrible writing habit now.

The rest of this section is going to explain further in-depth what make a sentence passive and how to correct it into active voice. Exercises will be provided so you can work on eliminating passive voice from first-hand experience.

Let's break the first sentence down.

The ball was thrown from the 5-year-old boy in the stands.

In this sentence, the five-year-old boy is the subject, the ball is the object, thrown is the verb and in the stands is the prepositional phrase.

So who's doing the action in this sentence? The boy. But in the way this sentence is written, it looks like the ball is doing the action by itself. In order to make this sentence better, let's switch the sentence around and make it active.

The 5-year-old boy in the stands threw the ball.

If you study this sentence, you can see that it flows better this way. The subject is doing the action, which makes the sentence make more sense. As you can see, switching from passive to active voice isn't as difficult as it sounds. With a little bit of practice, you'll become a writer who uses excellent active voice without any difficulty.

Let's practice changing sentences from passive voice to active voice. The following are exercises that ask you to make the sentence into active voice. As you complete the exercises, pay close attention to how active voice improves your writing immensely. If you have trouble, answers are provided in the back of the book.

EXERCISE A: Passive Voice to Active Voice

A.1   The book was marked with highlighters by Jackie.

A.2   Sam's backpack was stolen by a mother raccoon in the woods.

A.3   A can of beans slipped from Samantha's fingers.

A.4   Under the tree acorns were picked by two little girls.

A.5   The cake was eaten by Ben on a sunny day.

EXERCISE A: Passive Voice to Active Voice

A.6   A tub of chocolate ice cream slipped from Jane's hands and fell down the hill.

A.7   Quivering from fear, every single paper flew out of Robert's hands on the stage.

A.8   Just over the mountain, rescue packages were thrown from a plane to mountain climbers.

A.9   Gunshots were heard in the distance from Kenny's shotgun.

A.10   A bowl of rice spilled on the ground because Walter tripped.

Hopefully you understand passive voice better than before. It will take time before you'll be able to recognize passive voice in your writing and change it into active voice during the editing process. After identifying passive voice constantly, you will start writing active voice without even thinking about it. Now let's move onto active voice and break it down further.

Active voice is when the subject performs the action denoted by a verb. In other words, active voice is the most effective way to convey your thoughts and words. Practicing using active voice will make all the difference in your writing style. This style of writing is expected in college and will make you an overall better writer.

Here are some examples of active voice below:

> Sally rode her Clydesdale horse on a beautiful horse trail.
> The chef cooked quail eggs for the first time for Michelle's wedding last Saturday.
> Ian called the cops when he saw that an old man was robbed on the street.

As you can see, the use of active voice makes sentences not only more powerful but also succinct. The sentences are quick to the point and convey the sentence's meaning. Using active voice is key to becoming a better writer. Professors and employers expect you to use active voice in all types of writing. After working through this chapter, hopefully you'll be able to use active voice on a regular basis.

Let's break down a sentence using active voice to determine further why it's the best way to write.

> Sally rode her Clydesdale horse on a beautiful horse trail.

This example is straightforward and conveys the sentence's topic and meaning; the verb connects the subject to the object, which makes it a great sentence. If this sentence was written in passive voice, then the object would be acting it out on the subject, which is incorrect. Let's break down another sentence.

> The chef cooked quail eggs for the first time for Michelle's wedding last Saturday.

The chef is the subject of the sentence, cooked is the verb and quail eggs is the object. This sentence is another great example of active voice. If this example had used passive voice, it would look like this:

> The quail eggs were cooked by the chef for the first time for Michelle's wedding last Saturday.

As you can see, the quail eggs are doing the action to the chef, which isn't correct. Active voice flows better and conveys your sentence's meaning correctly every time. Let's practice writing sentences using active voice and then identifying whether the sentence is using active or passive voice.

Below are blanks for you to create your own sentences using active voice. Take your time when writing these sentences. Examples are provided in the back of the book.

EXERCISE B: Active Voice
B.1   Jill, beets, yesterday, canned
B.2   laugh, joke, from a book, twins
B.3   Hector, Ajax, The Odyssey, read
B.4   British literature, the professor, taught
B.5   ice cream, in the afternoon, ate Bill and Jan

EXERCISE B: Active Voice

B.6   underneath the table, sat, the fat cat

B.7   Zachary and Ian, in the morning, kicked, soccer ball

B.8   quivered, the kitten, between the couch, from terror

B.9   Carrie, in the afternoon, the track, ran

B.10   in the neighborhood, Kyle, rode, bike

Below are sentences that use either active or passive voice. Circle either "active" or "passive" at the end of the sentence. Answers are included in the back of the book.

EXERCISE C: Active or Passive Voice

C.1 The bag was carried from Timmy's house to the school bake sale. (Active/Passive)

C.2 After the birthday party on Sunday, Isabelle visited her grandma and grandpa. (Active/Passive)

C.3 A web of spiders fell onto Miss Rosaline's head in the forest. (Active/Passive)

C.4 Other than that, the pie was eaten by Jimmy in less than five minutes. (Active/Passive)

C.5 I saw Caroline the other day and said that you missed going to tea with her. (Active/Passive)

C.6 Considering the consequences, I'm still glad I went to the beach today even though I'm now sunburnt. (Active/Passive)

C.7 Even though you take ballet, hip-hop class is really difficult for you. (Active/Passive)

C.8 When I go to Jenny's house, a plate of cookies is always offered to me by her mom. (Active/Passive)

C.9 You can't eat that before we have dinner, Jameson. (Active/Passive)

C.10 Can you let me know when you land safely in San Francisco tonight? (Active/Passive)

After working through those exercises, active voice should be very familiar to you now. The best way to write more effectively is to read and work on exercises, so keep reading as much material as you can. Using active voice will transform your writing and impress your professors, colleagues and employers.

Conclusion

This chapter may have been difficult and somewhat tedious, but understanding the basics of active voice is vital to great writing. As a short review, we learned the definitions of active voice and passive voice, looked at examples of both and then worked on exercises. Active voice is one of the best ways to improve your writing. If you're still struggling with active voice, then re-work through this chapter again. If you feel very familiar now with using active voice, then let's move on to the next chapter: parallel structure in sentences.

"Writing is an act of faith, not a trick of grammar."

- E.B. WHITE

CHAPTER 18
Parallel Structure

Parallel structure is another essential building block to great writing. You may think that it's not an essential part of writing (let alone a sentence), then you are mistaken. This writing mechanic improves the form of your writing and how readers perceive it, too. If you remember the rules and work thoroughly through this chapter, then you'll quickly master parallel structure. Let's dive into the chapter now.

Parallel structure, also known as parallelism, connects one or more sentences of similar phrases or clauses that have the same grammatical structure. In other words, this writing mechanic helps make complicated sentences flow more smoothly.

Parallel structure improves your sentence by:

- Economy
- Clarity
- Equality

With so many important aspects, it's important that you understand what parallel structure and why's important to use correctly.

Here are some examples below:

> **Your business** and **its growth** have helped this town's economy boost this year.
>
> Rebecca cooked **turkey, gravy, cranberry sauce, mashed potatoes, and green beans for Thanksgiving this year**.
>
> Scott told me that he prefers **writing** rather than **reading**.
>
> **To enjoy** wine is **to savor** the flavor slowly.
>
> Penelope **not only hates** peas but **she also hates** lima beans, too.

After viewing these examples, you probably noticed that you either use or see parallel structure almost in everyday language. After working through these examples and exercises, you'll become a master of parallel structure yourself. But before we move onto the exercises, there are a few rules to understand. So let's dive in.

Rule #1: Parallel Structure with Coordinating Conjunctions

In regards to parallel structure, this rule is the most commonly used. Coordinating conjunctions connect a subject with its pronoun. Sometimes, young writers misuse coordinating conjunctions when connecting the subject to its pronoun. Here are some examples below:

> Incorrect: A school and what its faculty and staff have contribute to the school district's overall great performance.
>
> Correct: A school and its faculty and staff contribute to the school district's overall great performance.

Here are some other examples below:

What will Connie and her family do about moving to another city in just six months?

The dog and her puppy were lying in the sun this afternoon.

Aaron and the other boys were missing from math class.

As you can see, the subject and pronoun must use parallel structure in order to make sense and be correct. If you practice at using parallel structure with coordinating conjunctions in this section, then you'll be able to master it quickly. Let's practice with a few exercises.

Below are exercises that ask you to create sentences using parallel structure with coordinating conjunctions. Random words are provided for you, so feel free to get creative with your sentences. Examples are provided in the back of the book.

EXERCISE A: Parallel Structure Rule 1 Sentences
A.1   Jamie, his, and, playing, trumpet, in the band
A.2   quill, Benjamin Franklin, and, letter, write
A.3   in the swimming pool, but, the dog

EXERCISE A: Parallel Structure Rule 1 Sentences
A.4　Rachel, diving, and, her, on a sunny day
A.5　On the other hand, and, Lena, drew
A.6　Sammy, Paul, and, his, dog, in the park
A.7　Behind the couch, rabbit, and, on Sunday morning
A.8　Xavier, Pokemon, play, his, Gameboy

EXERCISE A: Parallel Structure Rule 1 Sentences

A.9   In the backyard, Evan, loves, his

A.10   Fences, Wendy, auditorium, and, her

After working through these exercises, you can see that parallel structure is fairly easy. Once you study the examples and practice it, this writing mechanic isn't hard to master. Let's do one more exercise just to make sure you fully understand it.

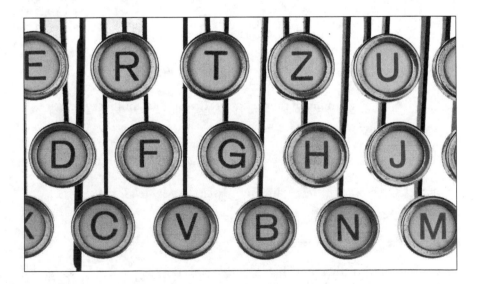

Below are exercises that are either using parallel structure or not. Circle "Yes" if the sentence is correct, or "No" if the sentence is incorrect. Answers are provided in the back of the book.

EXERCISE B: Parallel Structure Rule 1

B.1 Not only is Jordan going to the movies but also her brother. (Yes/No)

B.2 What to do with the professor and what is his new wife. (Yes/No)

B.3 On the other hand, Nathan and his brother-in-law got along last weekend. (Yes/No)

B.4 In the afternoon, Diane and her new puppy went to the dog park. (Yes/No)

B.5 Greg and their classmates are going to Disney World for spring break. (Yes/No)

B.6 Me and my girls are going to the spa today. (Yes/No)

B.7 Just because Henry is going doesn't mean he is. (Yes/No)

B.8 At the beginning of the night, the kitty and its mother were just outside the door. (Yes/No)

B.9 In general, Paula isn't close with what is her family. (Yes/No)

B.10 Dylan and the rest of his family went to Maine for the summer. (Yes/No)

Let's move onto the next rule if you understand the first one completely.

Rule #2: Parallel Structure with Elements in a List or Series

When writing sentences with lists or a series, parallel structure is vital. Not only does parallel structure make the sentence clearer but also more concise. Here are some more examples of parallel structure in lists or series below:

> This morning I cooked bacon, eggs, toast, and grits for my family.
>
> Kirk needs to buy paper, binders, pens, pencils, and highlighters for school next Monday.
>
> The southeast consists of Florida; Alabama; Louisiana; North Carolina; Georgia; South Carolina; Tennessee; and Kentucky.

Because lists and series appear in so many aspects of daily writing, it's important to relearn this rule so you aren't penalized for writing error. Let's practice using parallel structure in the exercises below.

Below are exercises that ask you to fix each sentence and use parallel structure instead. Take your time rewriting the sentences. Answers are provided in the back of the book.

EXERCISE C: Parallel Structure Rule 2 Sentences

C.1 Can you peel the potatoes, scrubbing the floor and taking out the trash for me?

EXERCISE C: Parallel Structure Rule 2 Sentences

C.2   Do you suggest switching math classes, take AP history and finish yearbook class?

C.3   After swimming, George also loves to bike and rowing.

C.4   Quickly take this food to Aunt Millie's house and baking the rest of these cookies there.

C.5   Other than that, the test was simple and flying by quickly.

C.6   Anderson wanted to stir the soup while talking to Pam on the phone.

EXERCISE C: Parallel Structure Rule 2 Sentences

C.7   In order to fix the bike, Jenny was driving to the nearest store.

C.8   To be great at running and jump hurdles well, you need to practice every day.

C.9   Derek is the leading rebounder and shooting player on the basketball team.

C.10   Just because I'm short and wider than you doesn't mean I'm not as beautiful as you.

Apart from memorizing this rule, there is one controversial exception that many writer—good and bad—argue over: the oxford comma.

The *oxford comma* is an optional comma that goes before the last item in a sentence. Critics, scholars, professors and writers argue over whether people should use it in sentences or not. In a college setting, some professors prefer you to use it; whereas others prefer you not to. However, it's good to know what the oxford comma is and when you should use it.

Here are some examples below:

> Option 1: Dusty the cat loves to hide beneath the couch, under the chair, or outside in the shed.
>
> Option 2: Dusty the cat loves to hide beneath the couch, under the chair or outside in the shed.
>
> Option 1: After the race this morning, all I want to do is eat some food, take a shower, and sleep.
>
> Option 2: After the race this morning, all I want to do is eat some food, take a shower and sleep.

Understanding and using the oxford comma correctly is fairly easy, but let's do a few exercises any way.

The following are exercises that ask you to insert commas into the sentences correctly. Answers are provided in the back of the book.

EXERCISE D: Parallel Structure Rule 2

D.1   I think the contestants on *American Idol* are awesome hilarious and talented.

D.2   Brent loves playing rugby because it's competitive exhilarating and rough.

D.3   Even though it's freezing out muddy and raining, I still love hiking during this time of year.

D.4   Either he's too busy doesn't know what's going on or just isn't interested in helping us out today.

D.5   Can we decide whether we are going to France Italy or Spain for vacation this summer?

D.6   When will Hannah finish the laundry her homework and go to ballet practice?

D.7   Quickly take the casserole out set the table and pour drinks for our guests.

D.8   Over the hill through the woods and under the bridge is where Mr. Toad's house is.

D.9   In the evening I'm taking Katie Emma and Christie to their dance recital.

D.10 Andrea took James' backpack calculator and pencils to his exam for him.

Using parallel structure, along with the oxford comma, is quite easy once you practice it. Let's move onto the next rule for parallel structure.

Rule #3: Parallel Structure with Comparison

When using comparison in sentences, you make use parallel structure in order for the sentence to make sense to the reader. Sometimes you don't notice that you're not using parallel structure, so make sure you proof your writing and correct it. Let's work through this rule and memorize it later for use.

Here are some examples below:

Incorrect: I enjoy biking rather than to rock climb.
Correct: I enjoy biking rather than rock climbing.

Incorrect: Fiona offered cake rather than cooking a real meal for us.
Correct: Fiona offered cake rather than a real meal.

Below are sentences that are either correct or incorrect. Circle true or false if the sentence is one or the other.

EXERCISE E: Parallel Structure Rule 3

E.1 I'd rather stay in and watch movies instead of running in this exhausting heat. (True/False)

E.2 Can you fix the faucet rather than sit around and watch TV all day? (True/False)

E.3 Little did she know that he'd rather be at home playing video games instead of watching her perform at the dance competition. (True/False)

E.4 Would you rather eat Brussel sprouts or salad for dinner? (True/False)

EXERCISE E: Parallel Structure Rule 3

E.5 On the bright side, I'd rather be stuck in traffic with you instead of someone else. (True/False)

E.6 Just in case you forgot, tomatoes are a fruit rather than a vegetable. (True/False)

E.7 Real or not, I prefer Gryffindor instead of Hufflepuff. (True/False)

E.8 When you take your final exam, contemplate each question rather than skimming through the entire test to get it over with. (True/False)

E.9 I'd rather sit in the shade then running all over the field and play flag football. (True/False)

E.10 Lily prefers to sit with us instead of her younger, annoying brother. (True/False)

After mastering parallel structure with comparisons, then you'll have every rule memorized and mastered altogether. Learning how to use parallel structure is pretty simple, so let's move onto the last rule: parallel structure with correlative conjunctions.

Rule #4: Parallel Structure with Correlative Conjunctions

Using parallel structure with correlative conjunctions is also another rule to keep in mind while writing. It's very easy to misuse parallel structure, so be aware of this when writing. In everyday speech, you and your friends may misuse it and not even notice that it's wrong; but in your writing, proof your work and correct it. Let's work through this last rule before we move onto the next chapter.

Here are some examples below:

> Incorrect: Not only do I love glitter, but also painting with it.
>
> Correct: Not only do I love glitter, but I also love painting with it.
>
> Incorrect: Will you assist me to the bathroom, so pinning my dress up won't be seen by other people?
>
> Correct: Will you assist me to the bathroom, so you can pin my dress up?

As you can see, using parallel structure has a similar pattern that will help you not only become a better writer, but will also help your readers understand your work better. Let's practice using parallel structure with correlative conjunctions so you can master this last rule and memorize it for the future.

Below are exercises that require you write sentences using parallel structure with correlating conjunctions. Feel free to get creative with your answers. Examples are provided in the back of the book.

EXERCISE F: Parallel Structure Rule 4
F.1   but, Orphelia, dog, sits
F.2   and, winning, George, trophy

EXERCISE F: Parallel Structure Rule 4

F.3   so, gorge, climb, the three brothers

F.4   also, Ian, peanut butter, jelly

F.5   because, kayaking, cliff diving, Dan

F.6   then, Jackie, banana pudding, chocolate

F.7   and, summer, winter, seasons

EXERCISE F: Parallel Structure Rule 4
F.8   so, I, cooking, cleaning
F.9   but, kite, Sally, park
F.10   because, Yolanda, writing, reading

Conclusion

Congratulations – you relearned all the rules of parallel structure. You probably feel like you're a master of it now. Although it was tedious to work through and memorize, parallel structure improves your writing in a profound way. Parallel structure helps you convey your message better and become a concise writer. If you feel comfortable with parallel structure, then let's move onto the next chapter: transitional devices.

> "Be able to correctly pronounce the words you would like to speak and have excellent spoken grammar."
>
> **- MARILYN VOS SAVANT**

CHAPTER 19
Transitional Devices

As mentioned in the last chapter, transitional devices are another vital part of great writing. This writing mechanic takes adequate writing and turns it into great writing. Especially in argumentative or persuasive writing, transitional devices help connect different paragraphs in an essay and make the piece flow better. In this chapter, you will learn what transitional devices are, view some examples of them and practice using them in your own writing.

Transitional devices are words or phrases that either introduce a sentence or help connect one thought to another. Once you've mastered the grammar basics and writing mechanics, transitional devices are the finishing touch on perfecting your writing. This chapter is very important to study, so take your time working through each definition, example and exercise. (See how I eliminated the oxford comma there?)

In a nutshell, transitional devices improve your writing by:

- Introducing a sentence or thought
- Connecting two or more thoughts
- Making your entire piece more cohesive rather than jumbled

To understand transitional devices better, let's look at are some examples below:

> **In order for this to work,** the bee must pollenate the flower before a certain period of time.
>
> **Thus,** the chicken is smarter than most humans think.
>
> **In conclusion,** the themes in Jane Eyre include male resistance, redemption and female abuse.

If you read these sentences without their transitional devices, then they would lose some of their power and meaning. Transitional devices make your sentences (and writing in general) come to life. Let's take a look at some of the transitional devices and their meanings.

Here are some transitional devices below. Not all transitional devices are listed here, but the most common are. These can serve as a chart for you to memorize which transitional devices you want to use in your writing (Courtesy of Purdue OWL):

- To Add: and, again, in addition, lastly, what's more, moreover, nor, too, next, equally important, besides, and then, finally, further, furthermore, first

- To Compare: whereas, but, although, in contrast, after all, meanwhile, however, on the contrary, by comparison, compared to, yet, on the other hand, however, nonetheless, nevertheless

- To Prove: because, for, since, obviously, in any case, indeed, in fact, evidently, technically

- To Show Exception: yet, still, sometimes, despite, once in a while, nonetheless

- To Show Time: immediately, soon, next, then, later, previously, after a few days, after a few hours, before

- To Repeat: as stated, as previously mentioned, as noted, in a nutshell
- To Emphasize: absolutely, definitely, without a doubt, emphatically, positively, naturally, in fact, in any case, obviously, extremely, always
- To Show Sequence: thus, simultaneously, consequently, afterward, finally, following this, in result
- To Conclude/Summarize: in summarization, as a result, accordingly, hence, thus, therefore, as shown
- To Give An Example: for instance, on this occasion, in this scenario, to demonstrate, for example

Although this is an exhaustive list, there are other transitional devices than the ones listed here. You probably recognize these and remember how they enhanced the writing that you saw them in. Before we dive into exercises, let's go over a few questions to remember when and where to use transitional devices. If you can memorize these questions and ask them to yourself while editing your work, then your writing will improve immensely.

Question #1: Am I writing a lengthy work that asks me to present a conclusion?

If the answer is yes to this question, then transitional devices are needed. If you're writing an email or another short piece of work, then you probably don't need them. Let's look at an example of this.

> I went to the farmers market because I had no groceries.
>
> As a result, I went to the farmers market because I had no groceries.

As you can see, the transitional device isn't really needed in this sentence because it explains itself already. When certain words or phrases aren't required in a sentence, it's best to eliminate them for concise, clear writing.

Question #2: Where should I insert the transitional device in this sentence?

Typically, writers use transitional devices in the beginning of sentences, but that doesn't necessarily mean that's the only correct way you can use them. There are tons of other ways in how you can use them. Let's look at some examples below.

> As a result, there are no aliens on this planet because of oxygen.
>
> There are no aliens on this planet because of oxygen, as a result.

You can even use insert the transitional device in the middle of the sentence, too.

> Heathcliff, however, creates sympathy in readers by the end of the novel.
>
> However, Heathcliff creates sympathy in the reader by the end of the novel.
>
> Heathcliff creates sympathy in the reader by the end of the novel, however.

It's up to you, the writer, to insert the transitional device wherever into the sentence. You should put it where it makes the most sense. Before you settle on where you put it, switch it around to see if you like one position more than the other.

Question #3: Does the transitional device add any significance to this sentence?

After using a transitional device in the sentence, you should ask yourself whether it adds any significance or not. If it doesn't, then you can either use another one or eliminate it from the sentence entirely. Let's look at the following sentence:

To be exact, I finished the race in 1 hour, 13 minutes and 8 seconds.

I finished the race in 1 hour, 13 minutes and 8 seconds.

Does it enhance the sentence? In this scenario, yes it does. But, on the other hand, the sentence would make just as much sense without it. Let's look at a few more examples.

In the end, the momma bird rescues her eggs from falling out of the nest.

The momma bird rescues her eggs from falling out of the nest.

In this context, the transitional device is essential. Without it, the sentence lacks meaning and purpose. Yes, you can use the sentence without it, but it won't be as powerful as it could be with this transitional device.

Other than that, Penny the dachshund is being potty-trained well.

Penny the dachshund is being potty-trained well.

Once again, the transitional device is vital to this sentence. In the first sentence, Penny the dachshund makes mistake but is overall doing well being potty-trained. In the other sentence, Penny seems like she is doing really well at being potty-trained. The transitional device adds so much meaning to this sentence.

Question #4: Am I using the correct transitional device in this sentence?

Sometimes, you may accidently use the wrong transitional device in a sentence, and that's okay. Recognizing that you're using the device is great when you identify it in the editing process. Let's look at a few examples that require different transitional devices.

> Since I'm not going to the national championship game anymore, I'll go to prom with my friends.

"Since" is the wrong transitional device to use in this sentence; "because" is a better fit instead. Since correlates with time, whereas because correlates with cause and effect.

> Because I'm not going to the national championship game anymore, I'll go to prom with my friends.

This sentence reads better with "because" added in. That's why it's always great to edit your work before you're finished with it. Let's look at one more example.

> However, Justine isn't as into babysitting her siblings as much as she used to.

This transitional device is great, but using another one would make it better. Here's one below:

> As a result, Justine isn't as into babysitting her siblings as much as she used to.

This device clarifies the sentence better and also gives more context to the meaning. After working through all these questions and examples, now it's time to practice them in exercises.

The following are exercises that ask you circle the transitional devices in the sentence. Answers are provided in the back of the book if you want to check your work or if you're stuck on an exercise.

EXERCISE A: Transitional Devices

A.1   For instance, I can do two back flips before diving into the swimming pool.

A.2   I love the cold but the summer is my favorite season in contrast.

A.3   Harold can no longer participate in P.E. class, as a result.

A.4   Obviously, Ursula was the bad character in *The Little Mermaid.*

A.5   Gina is attached to her mother, naturally.

A.6   I am, in fact, playing the leading protagonist in the new play at school.

A.7   Yet, I can't seem to go to sleep at night with everything that's been going on.

A.8   Pay attention to the test's meticulous directions, as stated.

A.9   In addition, add the chocolate frosting when the cake has cooled for an hour.

A.10 Evidently, you don't care whether I make the cheerleading team or not.

Hopefully, finding the transitional devices was fairly easy for you. Just so you fully understand transitional devices, practice writing your own sentences using them.

The following are exercises that require you to write sentences using transitional devices. Free feel to get as creative as you want. Examples are provided in the back of the book.

EXERCISE B: Sentences Using Transitional Devices

B.1   once in a while, Jane, reads, anime books

B.2   to demonstrate, the twin girls, hopscotch, love

B.3   since, running, shoes, worn out

B.4   sometimes, over the couch, Derek, lays

B.5   indeed, quail eggs, delicacy, countries

EXERCISE B: Sentences Using Transitional Devices

B.6   in fact, jogging, knees, hurts

B.7   on the contrary, you, kicked, dodgeball

B.8   technically, Sam, went, movies

B.9   as a result, can't, Aspen, skiing

B.10   moreover, jaguars, fastest, animals

Hopefully, you're a master of transitional devices by this point. If you're still struggling with them, then go back through this chapter and re-work it. Transitional devices can truly make or break your sentences, so take your time when mastering them.

Conclusion

As you can see, transitional devices are essential to great writing. With practice and reading, take notice of how great writers—contemporary or classic—use transitional devices. Also, take a look at college essays or any other type of persuasive writing. How do the transitional devices improve the writer's overall writing and tone? Can you insert a different transitional device? Is the transitional device even necessary? Study how they are used in all types of writing.

In summarization, transitional devices:

- clarify a sentence's meaning
- adds context to a sentence
- boosts your writing overall

Congratulations on making it through this chapter. Before you start working through the writing process, there is one more chapter to work through in this section that will help you master your writing: sentence clarity.

"The road to hell is paved with adverbs."

- STEPHEN KING

CHAPTER 20
Sentence Clarity

Sentence clarity is another important writing mechanic that makes you a great writer. When your writing isn't clear, then the reader is lost and confused about what message you're trying to convey. Even with perfect grammar and writing mechanic, your writing can be useless without sentence clarity. Making sure that your writing is cohesive is so vital.

Sentence clarity is a process of making sure your sentence is concise, clear and communicative. Between eliminating useless phrases, dangling modifiers and everything else that weakens your writing, sentence clarity takes practice and perseverance to master.

Even the literary greats struggled with sentence clarity through out their career. It may take you years to fully master sentence clarity, but it's always best to start now rather than later. After going through this chapter, hopefully you'll be able to identify sentence clarity in your own writing.

When clarifying your writing, there are a few factors to consider, such as:

- Dangling modifiers that hang off sentences
- Run-on sentences

- Useless phrases and words
- Words that don't make sense
- Unnecessary adverbs or adjectives

There are tons of other factors that clutter sentences and pieces of work, so these are just a few of what you should be aware of and avoid altogether. Let's go over a few rules, questions you should ask yourself in order to clarify your writing and exercises that will help you become a better writer.

Rule #1: Avoid misplaced (also known as dangling) modifiers.

Using misplaced modifiers is a very common error. Identifying them in your work is key to rewriting and making your writing better. You can also easily correct the sentence by putting it

Here are some examples below:

Wrong: Can you put the carton of eggs that we got this afternoon in the refrigerator?

Correct: Can you put the carton of eggs in the refrigerator that we got this afternoon?

Wrong: The couch needs to be cleaned in the living room.

Correct: The couch in the living room needs to be cleaned.

As a commonly used error, look over your writing and correct any misused modifiers in your writing. It's very easy to fix this mistake once you can easily identify it. However, most writers don't notice that the modifier is misplaced in the sentence, so pay attention to them when editing your work.

Rule #2: Watch out for wordiness and redundancy.

Using wordiness and redundancy is one of the most common errors in writing. Writers, especially beginners, believe that's it's best to write as much as they can in. However, this logic is completely false. Sometimes (as cliché as this is to say), less is more. You may be confused by that, but it's nonetheless true.

The best way to eliminate wordiness or redundancy is through editing. But once you're a great writer, you'll eliminate these two errors even before you write a single word. As you become a better editor, you'll become a better writer in general and "see" mistakes in your head before writing it down.

Here are some examples below:

> Incorrect: Whether or not you want to go to the gym, you have to go with me.
> Correct: Whether you want to go to the gym, you're going with me.
>
> Incorrect: Can you please re-send the document via email again?
> Correct: Can you please re-send the document via email?

When you read the incorrect examples, you probably thought to yourself, *Those sentences can't be redundant or wordy, right?* Unfortunately, yes they are. People are redundant in their everyday conversation, so those sentences probably sound correct to you. It's important to check your work and make sure that you aren't being redundant or too wordy. Professors expect you to be concise, fluent with your words and exquisite in your language.

Rule #3: Make your tense and voice shifts flow.

When writing, you probably don't ay attention to your sentence's tense shift and voice shift. You may accidently switch to a different tense while writing because you're so focused on the writing process. However, perfect sentence clarity is achieved when your sentence's tense and word choice remains the same throughout.

Here are some examples below:

> *Incorrect:* Janice loved going to the movies, but loves tanning at the beach.
>
> *Correct:* Janice loves going to the movies, but loves tanning at the beach.

> *Incorrect:* He raced his toy car yesterday and wins every time he races.
>
> *Correct:* He raced his toy car yesterday and won like he always does.

> *Incorrect:* The breeze drifted in the air, and the trees swayed in the breeze.
>
> *Correct:* The breeze drifted in air and swayed the trees.

> *Incorrect:* Hannah ate ice cream, and the ice cream was melting.
>
> *Correct:* Hannah's ice cream was melting.

As you can see, the voice and tense shifted in the incorrect sentences. Not only will your sentence lack cohesiveness, but will also confuse the reader. When editing your work, examine your sentence for tense or voice shifts.

After working through these rules, it's also best to ask yourself a few questions to help improve your writing and clarify your work. These questions will help you in all your writing endeavors. Try to memorize these questions because they will improve your writing.

Question #1: Can I make this sentence more concise?

This is the best question to ask yourself when examining your work. If you ask yourself this question, then you will most likely find all your writing errors and will be able to fix them. In order to practice and brush up on your editing skills, let's do a few practice exercises to help you identify wordy and concise sentences. Take your time as you work through each exercise, and feel free to go back through your work.

The following are exercises that are either too wordy or concise. Circle "wordy" or "concise" if the sentence needs editing or looks perfect. Answers are provided in the back of the book.

EXERCISE A: Sentence Clarity Question #1

A.1 Fred told Mindy who told John that he wanted you to come to his birthday party this weekend. (Wordy/Concise)

A.2 Mr. Collins told me that I was succinct, emphatic and persuasive in the argumentative essay I turned in last Tuesday. (Wordy/Concise)

A.3 Dean is one of the meanest people I have ever met in this world. (Wordy/Concise)

A.4 From what I hear, I think Matilda excels in almost every class except math. (Wordy/Concise)

A.5 At McAndrew's school, they make the students stay after school for extra test preparation. (Wordy/Concise)

A.6 Over the mountain lives an old hermit who doesn't like visitors. (Wordy/Concise)

A.7 On the radio, my favorite song played while cruising down the highway. (Wordy/Concise)

A.8 Polly the bird loves to sing songs and mimics my grandmother's voice sometimes. (Word/Concise)

A.9 The elephant, balancing on a beam, held an acrobat on its trunk and another one on its tail. (Wordy/Concise)

A.10 Football is America's most loved sport, but baseball is still my favorite, regardless. (Wordy/Concise)

Hopefully you're slowly becoming an editing expert and can catch wordiness and errors in not only your work but also in others. Let's now move onto the next question.

Question #2: Did I convey everything in my writing?

Besides writing errors, context is key to great writing. While editing your work, ask yourself, *Did I convey everything in this sentence and overall work?* If you notice that you're missing something, go back and rewrite that sentence until it's exactly what it needs to be. Let's practice with a few exercises to master this question.

The following are exercises that ask you to reexamine sentences that may or may not be missing a vital part. Circle "yes" or "no" if the sentence lacks or conveys meaning well. Answers are provided in the back of the book.

EXERCISE B: Sentence Clarity Question #2

B.1 Under the tree she put her backpack and clarinet case. (Yes/No)

B.2 In January, we plan on backpacking in Europe for three months. (Yes/No)

B.3 Kenna knew that I really wanted to go, so I'm made at her for that. (Yes/No)

B.4 Whether you think I should go or not. (Yes/No)

B.5 Benjamin doesn't know what to do for spring break. (Yes/No)

B.6 Quietly and cryptically throughout the house. (Yes/No)

B.7 Renee and her new baby were radiant at the party. (Yes/No)

B.8 Who wanted to go to the concert last night. (Yes/No)

B.9 Yesterday went pretty badly, if you ask me. (Yes/No)

B.10 Other than that, I really enjoyed his company. (Yes/No)

Even though this chapter focuses on sentence clarity, these exercises will also help you improve your editing skills, which is just as essential to writing as learning rules and grammar basics. After working through these exercises, let's move onto the next question.

Question #3: How can I improve my writing?

Even if you don't find any grammar or writing mistakes, it's always best to ask yourself, *how can I improve my writing?* Your sentence may be flawless and amazing, but there are ways to turn good and average writing into amazing writing. Let's practice identifying what's wrong in these sentences and suggesting what could make them better.

Below are exercises that ask you to examine sentences and identify what's wrong in the sentence. (For example, a sentence may have a misused modifier, so you would write "misused modifier in the blank.) Some sentences are correct, so leave the blank empty. Answers are provided in the back of the book.

EXERCISE C: Sentence Clarity Question #3
C.1 Same as you, Maria.
C.2 Into the forest she ran with her dog, Sydney.
C.3 Running into Marsha was really hard for me, considering how much she hurt my feelings.

EXERCISE C: Sentence Clarity Question #3

C.4   Over the top of the cake was the mini bride and groom.

C.5   Georgia never knew that her aunt was related to the queen of England!

C.6   Taylor, the new intern, didn't know.

C.7   Beneath the white ivory tower, standing underneath the towering silk trees.

C.8   Wherever you go, I go; wherever you stay, I stay.

EXERCISE C: Sentence Clarity Question #3

C.9   Put that milk in the refrigerator so it doesn't spoil.

C.10   Decide either now or later to accept the challenge.

You've made it through the first three questions, so let's work through the last two. Remember—take your time working through these questions so you can memorize and out them to use when editing your own writing.

Question #4: Did I proof my work enough?

Sometimes, you may think that you're done editing, but in reality you need to look over it more. This question refines your writing even more after reviewing your work already. Let's work on reviewing work that is already edited.

The following are exercises that ask you to examine sentences and determine whether any more editing is needed. Simply circle "yes" or "no" if the sentence needs improvement or not. Answers are provided in the back of the book.

EXERCISE D: Sentence Clarity Question #4

D.1 From the window, the night appears calm yet brooding. (Yes/No)

D.2 Just another day, another ordinary day here in Alabama. (Yes/No)

D.3 Under the sea lives aquatic animals and plant life. (Yes/No)

D.4 Xavier, the newest member on the soccer team, had to prove that he was good enough to join. (Yes/No)

D.5 Others were here, but now it's just you and me. (Yes/No)

D.6 Luckily, I brought an extra pair of goggles with me for the pool this afternoon. (Yes/No)

D.7 Question: does my new haircut look bad? (Yes/No)

D.8 Pick another outfit; I don't like that one. (Yes/No)

D.9 Another person said the same thing to me, but I just don't see it. (Yes/No)

D.10 For Cynthia, English class was super easy. (Yes/No)

If you are still struggling with these exercises, then check the answers in the back of the book and make sure you're fully understanding them. Let's move onto the last question now.

Question #5: Do I need to revisit any grammar or writing mechanic rules?

Even after editing and re-editing your work, you may have to ask yourself, *do I need to revisit any grammar or writing mechanic rules?* If you do, then go back through this chapter and rework through it. Let's practice one more time with some helpful exercises.

The following are exercises that ask you examine sentences and determine if any grammar or writing mechanic errors are in the sentence. Circle "yes" or "no" if there are or aren't any errors. Answers are provided in the back of the book.

EXERCISE E: Sentence Clarity Question #5

E.1   Work on your manners, Kent. (Yes/No)

E.2   Do what you need to do this class period, and I'll come check on you later. (Yes/No)

E.3   In the beginning of the year on the class field trip. (Yes/No)

E.4   Please let me extend my deadline for this paper, Mrs. Dennis. (Yes/No)

E.5   According to Victor, I didn't bring enough food for this road trip. (Yes/No)

E.6   Haley the highest jumper on the track team. (Yes/No)

E.7   Just because I don't know him doesn't mean we can't hang out. (Yes/No)

E.8   Because you know you need me to help you with this project. (Yes/No)

E.9   If you don't mind helping me move to my new apartment next Saturday. (Yes/No)

E.10   Could you please arrange the dinner table for your mother? (Yes/No)

As mentioned before, these questions will help you become the best editor and writer you can be if you put them to use. It will take some practice and time to memorize these, but you can do it. After working through this chapter, now you're ready to write!

Conclusion

After learning and memorizing the rules and questions, sentence clarity is one of the best editing processes to put your work through. From misused modifiers to unnecessary words, there are many grammar and writing mechanic errors that can deaden your work. But with practice, determination and patience, you'll become a great writer who writes flawless sentences. In a nutshell, sentence clarity is the key to making or breaking your work.

Congratulations—you've made it through the past two sections. Becoming a better writer takes time and patience, so completing this book alone speaks loud for your determination. After working through grammar basics to writing mechanics, you probably feel overwhelmed by all the material you've learned. However, you've mastered all the building blocks of writing, so you're ready to tackle the writing process.

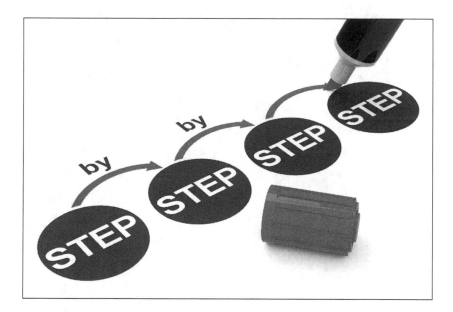

PART III:
The Writing Process

Congratulations—you've made it through the toughest chapters and sections of this book. Reviewing grammar and relearning writing mechanics isn't easy—and is quite laborious, too, if you're honest. But all great writing starts with the boring basics and builds itself up on solid sentences, creating succinct and thrilling writing.

Part 3 takes you through the entire writing process. Whether you are writing a letter to a friend or applying to college, this section will guide you through each essential part of writing, such as brainstorming, outlining, researching, writing, editing, and rewriting. It's important to work slowly through this section because it will make or break your overall writing.

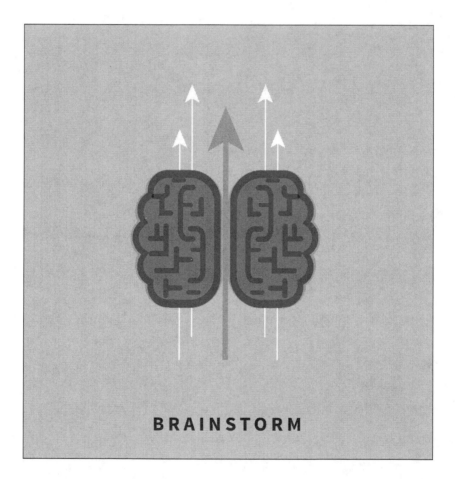

BRAINSTORM

CHAPTER 21

Brainstorming

Great writing doesn't just happen through correct grammar and stylistic choices. Flawless writing requires a thorough process of laying out the essay's (or another piece of written work) purpose and how you're going to convey that purpose to the reader in a straight-forward, easy-to-comprehend manner.

Before you sit down and start writing, the first step you should take is to brainstorm what you're going to write. Brainstorming is one of the most important steps to get the ball rolling in your writing. It not only lays out what you'll be writing about, but also helps you stick to your end goal.

This chapter will take you step-by-step in the brainstorming process, as well as discuss different types of writing and brainstorming practices. Let's dive into brainstorming now.

The *brainstorming process* includes putting on your creative thinking cap and mapping out what you're going to write. Brainstorming can be as simple as jotting down a few sentences to taking a few days to outline and organize all the content you want include in your writing. This chapter will take you through the basic steps of brainstorming and how it helps create better writing. It's up to you to determine whether the brainstorming process should take a couple of minutes or couple of days.

Before we begin, there are many ways to start your brainstorming process, but let's discuss the different types of writing before working through the brainstorming process. If you're writing a one-page personal essay or 20-page research paper, the brainstorming process will vary. Let's briefly go over each type of writing.

*A **narrative/personal essay*** is one of the most basic types of writing that you've already learned and will use throughout your lifetime. This type of essay is required for most college applications. Writing a strong personal essay is vital for getting accepted into college. A personal essay not only shows who you are as a person but also how well you write.

*An **expository essay*** is an essay that informs or explains a subject to the reader, such as teaching someone how to create a Facebook account or how ice is formed from water. Expository essays aren't very common types of writing, but it's good to understand what they are and how to write them. You probably read expository writing daily, but don't realize it.

*A **descriptive essay*** uses all five senses (taste, touch, smell, sound and feel) to paint a picture for the reader. Descriptive writing is used mainly in features, novels and other creative pieces. This type of writing has more freedom and creativity versus other types. Generally, descriptive essays are the most popular writing style due to its fun, creative process.

*A **persuasive/argumentative essay*** is a piece of writing that makes a claim or statement, then backs up that point throughout the rest of essay. Persuasive and argumentative essays typically are required in most high school English curriculum and also in college. Learning how to write effective persuasive and argumentative essays is a great skill to have and will become useful throughout your life.

A research paper is one of the most difficult but rewarding types of writing. They require much preparation, writing and editing and can take up to weeks to complete. However, writing a research paper is obligatory and will come in handy when you write your college thesis. Writing a spectacular research paper is a sought-after skill that will impress professors and employers and will make you stand out from others. That's why it's important to become a skilled writer and learn how to write the best research papers.

We will practice brainstorming a topic, outlining and writing a research paper as an example for this entire section. We will take you through the steps of how to prepare and write the best research paper possible. Pay attention to each chapter, and implement all the grammar basics and building blocks you acquired in the previous chapters.

So, let's finally begin!

4 Types of Brainstorming

Before you begin brainstorming for your research paper, here are the 4 types of brainstorming that will help you come up with creative ideas and with the flow of your research paper. It's always important to brainstorm a broad idea at first because you can always refine your idea later on.

The topic we are going to use as an example for our research paper is about J.K. Rowling and her rise to literary fame. We'll set the required word count to 2,000 words to help us stay on track, too. The rest of Part 3 will focus on this topic and walk you through each step.

Let's briefly go over each type and view some examples.

Mind Mapping/Webbing

This type of brainstorming is one of the most popular types to use when coming up with a topic to write about. Using mind maps helps you visually map out your topic, thesis and points or evidence to back up your claim.

Students who learn visually will be more drawn to using mind maps. Being able to see the entire layout of their brainstorming helps them visualize what their research paper will look like. Let's look over a quick example of how to create your own mind map.

All you need is a piece of paper to create a useful mind map. In the middle, draw a circle and insert a broad word or topic to start off with.

For instance, we are writing about J.K. Rowling's rise to literary fame. In the middle circle, we'd write "J.K. Rowling" to start off the brainstorming session with a broad topic to bounce subtopics off of.

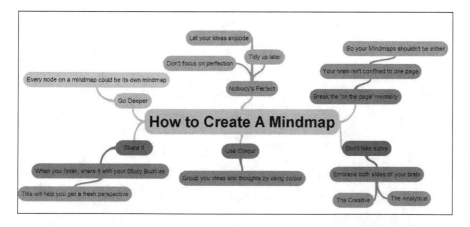

(Photo courtesy of Examtime.com)

The next bubbles that we'd fill in are "writing", "early life", "education" and "inspirations". Off those bubbles, create more bubbles to fill in more specific terms and so on. The more bubbles you create, the more specific your outline will become.

Hopefully this brainstorming method will help you think of specific subtopics you'll want to focus on in your research paper. Besides mind mapping, there are three other types of brainstorming, so let's explore those methods.

Outlining

Another popular type of brainstorming, outlining is a great way for students to brainstorm their research paper. Although the next chapter is dedicated entirely to outlining, using this brainstorming method helps organize which details and subtopics you'll want to focus on.

To begin outlining, you can either use a piece of paper or start a new document on your computer. Type or write out "J.K. Rowling", then work your way down every subtopic until you list out every possible detail you'd like included in your research paper.

Here is an example below:

J. K. Rowling: The Rise to Literary Fame

    I. Early Life

        A. Birth Place

        B. Childhood – Interests

        C. Childhood – Personality

    II. Early Career

        Early Writings

        Failures

        Obstacles

    III. The Harry Potter Series

As you can see, using an outline format for brainstorming helps organize your thoughts and come up with great subtopics for using in your research paper. This example is just a quick look at what a brainstorming outline should look like. You can go as in depth as you need to when brainstorming your paper topic, and outlining is a perfect way to do this.

Free writing

Free writing, another type of brainstorming, is a great method for avid writers and wordsmiths. If you're not particularly into outlining or mind mapping, then free writing is the method for you. This type of brainstorming is often the best to use for creative writing, but can be useful for research papers as well.

Free writing produces raw material that overcomes writer's block. A person writes continuously for a period of time and disregards spelling, a topic and grammar. Although this form of brainstorming isn't structured, free writing helps get the creative juices flowing, which helps your research paper in the long run.

Here is an example of free writing:

> J.K. Rowling wrote the Harry Potter series in the 1990s and rose to fame shortly after they were published. Inspired while on a train, Rowling wrote down the early beginnings of Harry Potter on a napkin in a café. Although the manuscript was rejected from several publishers, Rowling finally got one publisher to accept it. The authoress has one daughter and lives in Dublin.

Although this is a short example of free writing, this type of brainstorming is meant to produce great ideas from writing without limits. For example, the manuscript's multiple rejections from publishing houses would be a great subtopic to elaborate on. Free writing helps writers collect their scattered thoughts and organize them into workable ideas.

Listing/Bullet Points:

For extremely organized students, using lists or bullet points is another great brainstorming tactic. Whether you prefer numbers or just plain bullets, this type of brainstorming helps people organize their research paper's information.

Whether you jot down a few bullets or go more in depth, using lists and bullets keeps all your information in order and separated. You can even incorporate both into your brainstorming outline. What you choose to use is up to you.

Here is an example below:

J.K. Rowling

1. Early Life
   * Birth Place
   * Childhood – Interests
   * Childhood – Personality
2. Early Career
   * Early Writings
   * Failures
   * Obstacles
3. The Harry Potter Series

Using lists and bullets is similar to outlining, so students who like to keep their information organized will enjoy this form of brainstorming. Using this lists and bullets brainstorming method is a great way to get the ball rolling on prepping for your research paper.

Conclusion

All in all, finding the best brainstorming method is key to crafting your research paper. Try out a brainstorming method or two to see which one works the best for you. Prepping for your research paper is vital to writing the best paper that'll blow your teacher away.

As always, practice multiple brainstorming methods so you'll become a master at preparing for any research paper or thesis in an undergraduate or graduate program. The more you practice, the better you'll get.

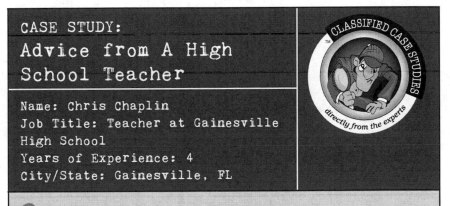

CASE STUDY:

Advice from A High School Teacher

Name: Chris Chaplin
Job Title: Teacher at Gainesville High School
Years of Experience: 4
City/State: Gainesville, FL

Q What are some of the most common grammar and writing mistakes you've seen?

Frequent grammar mistakes for my 10th-grade AP students include passive voice and homophone errors (they're/their/there, its/it's, too/two/to, etc...). Here is a common example of passive voice disrupting clarity: "An argument made on this topic is that a piece of literature be judged on its presentation of human existence." Here is a common example of a homophone error: "Its important that literature reflect human nature accurately in order for it to be considered a classic."

Q How do you try to improve/teach students how to use better grammar and writing styles?

When helping students correct common grammar errors, I pull out examples from their writing as well as self-generated examples. I spend about 10 minutes discussing the error and how it impedes clarity of expression. Then I model how to correct the error, eventually getting the minds of the students engaged by giving them to floor at the board to collaborate on solutions for other examples that I provide. Finally, after a day or two or working of practice correcting these errors, I unleash them to work collaboratively to edit and revise their own writings for these errors.

Q What do you recommend for students to do in order to improve on their own?

Students need to give themselves the time to really think about every word that they put on paper. They need to think about their writings as texts, just as any other texts that we read in an English class. I ask them to find someone to read their texts, someone who will call them out on clarity issues.

Q Why is it important for students (especially in high school) to have good grammar and writing skills?

Good grammar and writing enables a student to express their beliefs as citizens in practice. I always call students to prepare themselves for their responsibility to vote in the next few years. Being able to organize thinking into clear, concise writing helps a student to know what they truly know and believe.

Q Any additional advice for students?

Students, any human being, benefits when their writing is heard aloud by another person. This removes the writer's intentions from their executed use of language.

CHAPTER 22
Outlining

Outlining is one of the most important steps in preparing for writing your research paper. It's the key to keeping your research paper on track and completing your paper's "mission". This is one of the most important steps to take your time on. If you write a thorough, in-depth outline, then writing your rough draft will be much more easier for you.

An *outline* comes in different forms, which depend on your preference as a writer. There isn't a "best" way to outline, but the outlining form you choose should help you organize your research paper's topic.

This chapter will help you understand why outlines are necessary for research papers, organize your outline (whether you choose to use a bullet list, Roman numeral or written form) and check if your first completed outline is thoroughly finished. Let's begin.

Reasons Why Outlining is Essential

Before you write a personal essay, note to a friend or any other type of writing, you probably don't outline what you're going to write. However, when writing a research paper, it's vital to outline – in intricate detail – what the introduction, body and conclusion will consist of.

Outlining is essential for writing your research paper because:

1. An outline serves as the roadmap of writing your paper.

As mentioned, outlining is essentially the skeleton of your paper; it lays out the reasons or subtopics that will be stated throughout your entire paper. If you begin writing your research paper without an outline, your paper will lack focus and content.

2. An outline tells you how many research materials you'll need.

Once you've completed your outline, you will have the chance to see how much research and evidence your paper will need to back up claims made throughout the paper. For instance, you may only need a few sources if your paper is relatively short in length, or you may need about 10 research materials.

3. An outline points out whether you're missing any vital information before it's too late.

After writing your outline, glancing over it helps identify if you're missing any main points that should be included. Once again, catching this error now prevents you from making major changes to your research paper after the rough draft is completed.

Overall, outlining sets your research paper up for being great and completing the given prompt. With practice and patience, you'll become a great outliner, which eases the arduous rough draft process.

Creating an Outline

When creating your outline, it's important to determine to research paper's purpose and how you want to back up your claims. Feel free to be as detailed as you want in the outline. The more intricate your outline is, the more you have to work with.

Here are three points to keep in mind when you're creating your outline:

1. Determine your research paper's purpose.

It's a simple yet important question: *What's the purpose of my research paper?* Just start with the basics and work your way to a specific topic.

For example, we want to write a research paper about J.K. Rowling. To take it a step further, we want to focus on her writing career and how the Harry Potter series transformed her literary status. So our working title is going to be "J.K. Rowling's Magical Literary Journey".

This topic isn't too broad but also not too specific enough where we wouldn't be able to write enough about the subject.

2. Determine your audience.

After pinning down your paper's purpose, determine your audience. Are you writing for a teacher, or is your paper being read by your classmates? Once you've determined your audience, you can pinpoint what type of in-depth research and voice your paper must have.

For example, our paper is being written for an English class assignment, so the overall tone will be professional but also insert some flowery language to make the paper interesting.

Once you determine your audience, the style and tone of your outline will come more naturally. It's always important to know who you're writing for.

3. Develop your outline.

Now, you're ready to write your outline! Whether you want to use a bullet-point list, or Roman numerals, begin writing your outline. Take your time planning your outline and what you want to include in your paper.

Here is an example of an outline on writing about J.K. Rowling's writing career:

Working Title: J.K. Rowling: A Magical Writing Journey

I.   Introduction:

II. Paragraph Body #1: A Life-Changing Epiphany on A Delayed Train Ride

    A.   Delayed train from Manchester to London inspired Harry Potter

    B.   Started outlining for the next five years

III. Paragraph Body #2: How Loss Inspired the Making of Harry Potter

    A.   Mother's death

    B.   Divorce

    C.   Poverty

    D.   Book Rejections

IV. Paragraph Body #3: How 'The Boy Who Lived' Transformed Rowling's Literary Career

    A.   Creative Process: Creating the Harry Potter World

        1.   Thorough outlines

        2.   In-depth books

  B. Success

    1. Books

    2. Movies

  C. Inspiration

    1. Writers

    2. Readers

V. Paragraph Body #4: Life After Harry Potter: Rowling's Current Writing Career

  A. Harry Potter Extras

  B. Adult Books

    1. The Casual Vacancy, The Cuckoo's Calling and The Silkworm

VI. Conclusion: How J.K. Rowling Inspires Writers to Chase Their Dreams

  A. Charities

  B. Writing

  C. Inspiration

When you finish your outline, there is always a good chance you're going to rework or change something; it's just inevitable. However, it's important to spend your time making your outline the best it can be the first time so you can speed up the entire process.

Conclusion

Outlining your research paper not only helps make the writing process much easier, but also motivates you to write the best research paper possible. If you have a clear roadmap of what your research paper will look like, then it'll be that much easier to make it happen. Take your time outlining your research paper. This step is vital in making or breaking your rough draft.

Once you feel comfortable with your rough draft, let's move on to the next step: gathering your research materials.

CHAPTER 23

Gathering Your Research Materials

After creating a great outline, gathering a plethora of research materials is key to writing a fantastic research paper. Backing up your thesis requires great resources, so finding all the materials you need – whether it's online articles, journals, in-person interviews or reference books – will help cushion your paper and make it solid with facts.

This chapter will help you understand what research materials are, go through the different types, organizing and gathering everything you need to make a claim in your research paper, reevaluating if you have enough and how to properly cite them throughout the paper. Let's begin!

What are research materials, and why do I need them?

Research materials are documents, interviews, or any other type of written or spoken materials that serve as hard evidence for making a claim or statement. Typically, students use scholar articles and reports only and don't really use any other type of research materials.

Gathering the right amount of research materials is vital for supporting claims in your research paper. If you don't have enough research, then you won't have enough to write about and be able to support your paper. Make sure you take your time and gather enough articles and other research materials to make your paper great.

Step 1: Gathering Your Research Materials

In the digital age, gathering research materials is as easy as searching for scholarly articles and reports from your computer. Most articles can be accessed and immediately downloaded so you can scroll through them on your computer and highlight which parts you'd like included in your research paper.

However, students can still use resources, such as reference books and periodicals, that can be found and checked out at libraries. It's good to use online journals and physical books to include in your research paper.

Here are the different types of research materials and resources that will help you write a flawless research paper backed up with solid evidence.

Types of Research Materials

Reference books are physical books that can be checked out at libraries. They provide authoritative facts on all subject matters. Reference books aren't used as much anymore (due to the Internet), but they still serve as great resources for research papers.

Periodicals and journals are another resource for research papers. Typically printed in books, periodicals and journals can be found online now. These resources provide great evidence for research papers and reports.

Library databases provide students a plethora of reports, articles and more. You can essentially find an article on any topic you are writing about. Sometimes, there are unique articles and reports that will be a great asset for your research paper.

Here is a list of useful library databases:

- JSTOR

- Questia

- Project MUSE

Online publications are the most popular and useful resource for papers. These publications can include analytics reports, data sheets and any other statistics that might be useful and back up your paper's claims.

Scholarly articles and reports are publications written by scholars, researchers and others. They come in a variety of topics and serve as great resources for research papers. Generally, you can find scholarly articles in library databases and immediately download them to your computer to use them.

For example, when writing the research paper on J.K. Rowling's writing career, we would use biographical materials, some in-depth statistics and articles on the Harry Potter Series and hunt down any interviews of J.K. Rowling.

It's important to examine your research paper's topic and determine which types of research materials you'll need. If you're writing a scientific research paper, you'll want to use data reports, statistical evidence and also scholarly articles written on the same topic. Gathering an abundant research materials is always better than not gathering enough.

It may take you a couple of days or even weeks to find the right resources to include in your research paper. so start looking for research materials as soon as possible.

Step 2: Organizing Your Research Materials

Once you find all the research materials you need, organize the resources into groups. Knowing when and where you're going to use a resource will help you write your rough draft faster.

For example, when organizing research materials for the J.K. Rowling research paper, we would group them into categories: a Harry Potter category, current writing category, etc.

It's most likely that you'll use two to three resources for each section in your research paper, so highlighting, bookmarking and grouping the parts you're going to use will help you stay organized and form your claims.

This step won't take too long after you've read through all the resources and have determined which parts you'll use.

Step 3: Reevaluating If You Have Enough Research Materials

Once you've organized your research materials into categories, identify if you're missing any vital evidence for your paper. Taking the time to check if you need to find more resources will save you the hassle of going back to look for more articles or reports once you've completed your rough draft.

Here are some questions to ask yourself when evaluating whether you need to gather more or not.

"Does this research paper require more resources?"

If each reason, section or claim has sufficient evidence, then you probably have enough supportive materials. If you're writing a 2,000-word paper, then three to five resources are enough. If you're writing a 40-page thesis, then you'll want to include at least 10 or so resources. As mentioned, take your time to determine whether you have enough or not.

"Should I re-organize my research materials?"

Even if you have all the resources you need, check if they are all categorized and organized in the right sections. Sometimes, one resource should be included in other and vice versa. Make sure you organize your materials as good as you possibly can. This will help when you write your rough draft.

Step 4: How to Properly Include References and Citations in Your Research Paper

When you write your research paper, you must properly cite all research materials and resources used throughout. This is one of the hardest parts of writing any paper. Citing is a time-consuming, hard task, but it's vital that you understand how to do it well.

Bibliographies are lists of scholarly works and research included at the end of a research paper. They state what sources you used and can be referred to throughout the paper.

There are different types of citing styles, and it's important to know the difference.

Types of Citing Styles

MLA

The MLA (Modern Language Association) citation format is most commonly used in humanities-related research papers. This type of citing style requires writers to include references after citing a source and include bibliographies at the end of papers.

Here is an example of referring to a source in the paper:

> Although J.K. Rowling was delayed by a four-hour train ride from Manchester to London, the epiphany of Harry Potter popped into her mind, and she immediately began to jot down ideas (Parker, 23).

Here is an example of including a bibliography:

> "J.K. Rowling: A Life." *International Literacy Club.* Edna Parker, 15 June 2003. Web. 24 May 2009.

APA

The APA (American Psychological Association) citation and format style is generally used for science-based research papers. This type of citing style is very different from MLA and can be seen in business, nursing and other related papers.

Here is an example of referring to a source throughout the paper:

According to Reed (2004), "J.K. Rowling suffered from poverty when she divorced her husband and was left to fend for her and her daughter" (p. 27).

Here is an example of a bibliography:

Contributors' names (Last edited date). *Title of resource.* Retrieved from http://Web address for J.K. Rowling resource

Chicago

The Chicago Manual (16th edition) citation and format style is a method of documenting and formatting research papers. Typically, this citation style isn't used that much, compared to MLA and APA. However, it's still good to be familiar with this style.

Here is an example of referring to a source throughout the paper:

According to Lynne Warren, Rowling didn't always have an easy time of it:

From my perspective, it seems as if Ms. Rowling used the Harry Potter series to reflect her real-life situations (102).

Here is an example of a bibliography:

Warren, Lynne. "The Early Writings of J.K. Rowling." *Publishing Organization or Name of Website in Italics.* Publication date and/or access date if available. URL.

Note: For more information on the MLA citation and formatting, the Purdue OWL is great for helping you out:

https://owl.english.purdue.edu/owl/.

Conclusion

Although it takes a long time to search and find the best research materials, these resources will help you form your research paper better and have enough material to write as much as the writing assignment requires.

As a general rule, it's always better to gather too many materials rather than too little. The more you include in your research paper, the better your claims will be (and your grade is be higher, too!). Once you're done organizing your research resources, it's time to discuss one of the most inhibiting factors to writing: writer's block. Let's learn how to overcome it!

"Start writing, no matter what. The water does not flow until the faucet is turned on."

- LOUIS L'AMOUR

CHAPTER 24

Struggling With Writer's Block

Unfortunately, writer's block can strike at any time. Whether you are developing your thesis (which is discussed in the next chapter) or are re-writing your research paper for the seventh time (hopefully, this won't be you.), writer's block sucks all the creativity, motivation and drive out of you. From students to the literary greats, writer's block affects everyone, but there are ways to overcome it.

This chapter will help you understand what writer's block is, what forms they come in and ways to overcome writer's block.

What is writer's block?

Writer's block is the mental inability to write or come up with creative ideas. Whether you are writing a research paper or another creative project, writer's block can strike you at any time. However, it's best to combat writer's block head on, especially when you're on a deadline.

Determining what types of writer's block affect you and creating ways to overcome them will help you continue to write without any internal or external interference. If the literary greats are affected by it and can overcome it, then so can you.

What forms does writer's block come in?

Writer's block comes in various forms, such as mental, internal or external factors. Although most people don't think writer's block is a real condition, studies have shown that writer's block does in fact affect people's writing flow.

Here are some forms in which writer's block can affect you:

- **An author's own work**: You may have planned, prepped or thought about your research paper so much that when you sit down to write it, no words flow. Another potential issue is that your writing topic may not interest you or is a tough subject to write about. Becoming motivated to get started on your work is a very common form of writer's block.

- **Fear of failure**: Having the fear of not writing a great research paper and failing instead can startle many writers and cause them to have writer's block. Once they start writing a few words on the page, then this type of writer's block can go away; it's all mental for him or her.

- **Having a deadline**: Feeling pressured from a deadline can, believe it or not, cause writer's block. When a writer panics about having to do so much work in a small amount of time, it can discourage him or her. This type of writer's block is external.

- **External distractions**: This is probably the most common type of writer's block, especially for teens and students. External distractions, such as a cell phone, TV or even relationship problems, can cause writer's block. When your mind is solely preoccupied on another object or topic, this can decrease motivation and focus.

Some of these types of writer's block may affect you, but fortunately there are ways for overcoming them. Below are some creative outlets to get the ball rolling on your writing.

Types of creative ways to overcome writer's block

1. Step away from working on your research paper.

Yes, that's right: Step away from your paper. Although working on your paper is great, working on it for too long actually isn't good for you (or the paper in the long run). Taking breaks, and working at a slow, steady pace, helps your mind refocus and be more creative and alert with fresh ideas later on. So go watch a TV show or catch up with a friend – this is good for you and your paper!

2. Eliminate distractions.

There's probably something that's distracting you from working on your paper. It can be a talkative friend, your cell phone, TV, or even various conflicts in your life. Compartmentalize these, put them away and focus on your paper. Although writers think they can multi-task, it's not the best method to tackle your paper.

3. Freewrite anything you want.

Is your paper's topic sucking the soul out of you? Then write about something else – anything you want. Writing about random things or prompts will help you focus on another topic and get your creative thoughts rolling again. This method will help you write faster and conquer your paper.

4. Listen to music

Listening to music actually helps you write better and be inspired without re-alizing it. Whether you enjoy indie, classical or Top 40 music, create a playlist and start writing. Some writers believe that it improves their writing and helps them write for longer. So discover a new artist, or jam to an old one. Music will help you get started on your paper.

5. Read, read, read!

Reading is the best way to overcome writer's block and inspires writers to come up with new ideas. When famous writers get stuck on anything, they immediately submerge themselves into writing. Whether you want to catch up on your favorite author or new magazine issue, read all you want. This will help you when you sit down to write your research paper.

6. Create a routine.

Yes, this is actually the most ideal situation for writing your research paper. If you are a night person, then set aside a time to write for an hour at night. If you're a morning person, then set aside a time to write then. If you create a routine, you'll not only train your body and mind to get used to writing but also be productive and get so much work done.

7. Be inspired.

Surround yourself with what inspires you, whether that's inspirational quotes, music, books, motivational speeches, or hobbies. Boosting yourself with in-spiration will help you start writing and accomplish your task.

Having writer's block cramps your productivity and frustrates you, so eliminate it as soon as it strikes. If none of these ideas help you, try others. There is something out there that will help you become creative again and get you started writing.

Conclusion

Remember: writer's block can be overcome. Don't be frustrated with yourself if you can't write anything for a while. It happens to everyone. But if you try one of these tactics to get your creativity flowing again, then writer's block won't affect you anymore.

Once you've practiced a few ways to overcome writer's block, let's move on to the next chapter: developing your thesis before writing the rough draft.

CHAPTER 25

Developing Your Thesis/Topic

Just like outlining, your thesis is essentially the roadmap for your research paper. It steers your body paragraphs as well as the conclusion. Your thesis makes a claim that the rest of your research paper supports and makes it a true statement. However, writing a great thesis is one of the hardest parts in the writing process; even college students and adults struggle with creating a knockout thesis.

This chapter will help you understand what a thesis is, what makes a thesis a great one, and provides you with examples and steps on how to write a good thesis. Let's begin.

What is a thesis?

A *thesis* is a statement or theory that is put forward as a premise or proved true throughout the entirety of a paper or essay. It serves as the summary of your paper as well. If you write a clear, definitive thesis, then you won't have any problem writing an effective research paper or essay that executes all the points made in this statement.

Typically, the thesis is inserted at the end of your introduction, stating what the research paper will either persuade the reader or defend. Writing your paper's thesis will take up the majority of your time, believe it or not. Crafting the perfect thesis statement takes a lot of editing and re-writing.

Most students struggle will writing a thesis, let alone understanding what they even are. If you can master drafting up great thesis statements in a short amount of time, then you'll be ahead of the game in college. Take your time to write a killer thesis for your paper, and you'll impress your teachers and professors.

What makes a thesis a *good thesis?*

There are a few components to creating a great thesis. Your early draft, called a "working thesis", will undergo many revisions until its finalized form, but that's a completely normal process for all theses.

Your thesis will:

- Answer the prompt
- State why your conclusion is correct (include about three reasons/statements)
- Tell the reader what they will be reading.

However, these are just the minimum requirements of creating a great thesis. You must go above and beyond to craft a thesis statement that knocks it out of the park.

Here are some examples:

In "The Great Gatsby," the green light represents the American Dream and how its idealistic expectations create illogical hope, throw away all common sense, and ultimately, destroy a person.

Emily Brontë introduces Heathcliff in "Wuthering Heights" as a juxtaposition of Yorkshire life, the Earnshaws, and English society.

In her poem, "Mirrors," Sylvia Plath inserts autobiographical themes of her fear of growing old, failure in her writing career, and conforming to domestic duties that she wanted to desperately escape.

These examples show that there is a standard format for thesis statements, but they can vary as well. There isn't a "correct" way to write a thesis. Sometimes, you need to experiment with different styles to see which one fits in your research paper well.

Below are four steps of getting started on your thesis. Take your time, and be patient when writing. The more time and energy you put into your thesis, the better it will turn out in the end.

Step 1: Identify your topic.

For these steps, we are going to create a thesis about J.K. Rowling's writing career. The first step is identifying the topic. We have selected to write specifically about Rowling's writing career and how the Harry Potter series boomed her literary status.

Second, we want to focus on her career before Harry Potter, her career during Harry Potter's popularity and her writing career post-Harry Potter.

So, this is what our early thesis would look like:

J.K. Rowling's writing career, Harry Potter, struggle to get published, career is now flourishing, lived in poverty

Step 2: Write your thesis – without any editing

After jotting down a few ideas, just go ahead and write your thesis. Don't worry about whether it's good or not. To be honest, it probably won't be good, but that's okay. It gives you a chance to work with something and rewrite it to make it great.

Below is our (very) rough thesis draft:

> Due to J.K. Rowling's poverty status, numerous manuscript rejections, and other tragic life situations, she channeled all her struggles into the Harry Potter series, which made her one of the most beloved children's book writers of all time.

As you can see, this thesis is extremely rough, but includes all of our main points. After letting the thesis sit for a little bit (don't make yourself work on it tirelessly), take it out again and work on it.

Step 3: Refine your thesis

This is perhaps the most important step. Refining your thesis may take only revision – or 10. It depends on how complicated your thesis statement is going to be.

Here are a couple of revisions of our thesis:

> J.K. Rowling's writing career portrays a triumph of poverty, manuscript rejections, and tragic losses in her life.

> With the success of the Harry Potter series, J.K. Rowling's writing career portrays a triumph of poverty, manuscript rejections, and tragic losses in her life.

> With the success of the Harry Potter series and her own "rags to riches" story, J.K. Rowling's writing career portrays a triumph of poverty, manuscript rejections, and tragic losses in her life.

As you can see, we re-worked the thesis until we included all research paper's points, refined the language and made a compelling argument for the rest of the paper. You should re-work your thesis so it flows smoothly and makes a great case for your research paper.

Step 4: Repeat any step needed

After working through different thesis statements, we went with our last one:

> With the success of the Harry Potter series and her own "rags to riches" story, J.K. Rowling's writing career portrays a triumph of poverty, manuscript rejections, and tragic losses in her life.

As mentioned, repeat any step needed. If that means you need to regroup and go back to Step 1, then go back by all means. Taking the time to work on your thesis will make all the difference for your rough draft and final draft.

We suggest rewriting your thesis statement about three or four times until you think it's as good as it'll get. Once your rough draft is completed, you may want to go back and re-work your thesis later on, but that only happens in certain situations.

Conclusion

Your thesis is very important. Most teachers spend much of their time teaching students how to create and write a good thesis because it's one of the hardest steps to accomplish in the writing process. Hopefully this chapter helped you understand theses better and how to write a great one that leads your paper.

Now, after working through all the previous chapters, let's move on to the chapter you've been waiting for: writing your rough draft.

"Half my life is an act of revision."

- JOHN IRVING

CHAPTER 26
The Rough Draft

Writing your rough draft is a longest part of the writing process because you are writing and completing the entire work. Depending on the word count, a rough draft can take many hours (or several days) to finish. However, once you've completed it, you'll be proud of all the work you've accomplished. Your rough draft will serve as a work-in-progress for creating an incredible final paper that will please any teacher or professor.

This chapter will help you understand what a rough draft should look like, how to tackle different sections of your rough draft and questions you should ask yourself before finishing it.

"What is a rough draft supposed to look like?"

This is a very common question that almost all writers ask themselves. Rough drafts will vary for each writer as well.

A *rough draft* can come in many forms. Some writers believe rough drafts are just the "skeleton" version of a paper, whereas others believe it should include everything the final draft entails of. However, a rough draft isn't just the first time you write your research paper. You'll continuously work on many rough drafts until you complete your final draft.

Powering through your rough draft will take determination and an ample amount of time, so give yourself a set of goals to accomplish that are doable. Let's run through our checklist below before we get started:

Rough Draft Checklist

Before you begin writing your rough draft, make sure you have everything aligned. Here is a quick checklist of some things you may need when writing your rough draft:

- <u>Give yourself a nice, clean space to write:</u> When you're in the throes of writing, you'll need a great, spacious table where you can spread out any notes, papers, your computer, and any other miscellaneous items you'll need when writing.

- <u>Put away all distractions:</u> Yes, turn out the TV, stow away your phone and anything else that will disturb you from writing. The more focus you have, the better (and quicker) the rough draft writing process will be.

- <u>Have a cup of coffee, bottled water and snacks with you while you write:</u> You'll get exhausted while writing your rough draft (especially depending on the length), so make sure you have something to sustain you. Try to avoid sugary, high-caffeinated drinks because you'll just crash and not being able to finish your rough draft.

- <u>Bring all your notes, outlines and other research materials:</u> You're going to need all of the research materials you gathered while you write your rough draft as a reference for guiding each section. The more you organize your materials, the faster you'll be able to finish writing your research paper.

- <u>Bring headphones to listen to music or just block out noise:</u> Although some people may discourage you to not listen to music while writing, this theory depends on the writer. Sometimes, listening to music encourages mental creativity, whereas it distracts others. It's up to you to decide whether you need music to help you write your rough draft.

- <u>Give yourself an entire day or timed writing periods broken over the span of a few days to finish your rough draft:</u> Whether you want to complete your rough draft in one sitting, or want to spread it out over a couple of days, create a plan of action and stick to it. This will help keep ideas fresh in your mind and also complete your rough draft very quickly.

Once you've prepped your writing area (either at home, the library or a coffee shop), it's time to tackle the rough draft. Let's dive in.

Tackling Each Section in Your Rough Draft

It's the moment you've been waiting for: writing your rough draft. This section breaks down each part so you can write the best rough draft the first time. Take your time writing each section so you don't have to rewrite your rough draft over and over.

The Introduction

The introduction consists of presenting your topic, evidence and thesis to the reader. Typically, this portion of the rough draft is kept quite short compared to the rest of the research paper. Length-wise, it's only a paragraph long.

Here is an example of a great introduction:

> Becoming a literary icon usually happens in an author's posthumous life. For J.K. Rowling, it happened almost overnight. After selling more than 400 million copies of the Harry Potter books and having the second largest grossing film series, Rowling quickly became the one of the most

beloved children's author of all time. However, the authoress faced a series of devastating trials while writing the early beginnings of the magical world. With the success of the Harry Potter series and her own "rags to riches" story, J.K. Rowling's writing career portrays a triumph of poverty, manuscript rejections, and tragic losses in her life.

Although this introduction is rather short, it's quick, to the point and fully lays out what the rest of the research paper is going to be about. Depending on how long your writing assignment is, a concise introduction is always preferred.

The Body of your Research Paper

This is where you'll write the majority of your research paper. In the body paragraphs, you'll essentially defend your thesis with evidence and strong reasoning. These sections will probably give you the most trouble (and ones you'll work on the most when you rewrite your rough draft). Let's begin writing these paragraphs.

Body Paragraph #1: Loss & Abandonment in Rowling's Life

In this body paragraph, the main themes are loss and abandonment in Rowling's early writing career. When you're including the top themes or pieces of evidence that back up your claim, make sure you pick the three or four strongest ones. These will make your research paper and thesis stronger.

Here is an example below:

When the inception of Harry Potter occurred, Rowling experienced loss and abandonment in her life, which eventually played a vital role in the main character's life. The first tragic loss was Rowling's mother. She passed away right before Rowling told her about a new book idea she conjured. Soon after, Rowling experienced a heightened sense of abandonment. Her husband left and divorced her, leaving Rowling and her young daughter penniless. However, Rowling kept outlining and sketching out the early works of the Harry Potter series, infusing personal life experiences into some of the most beloved characters of all time.

Body Paragraph #2: Poverty & Welfare

This paragraph includes themes about poverty, welfare, and how they influenced Rowling's writing. Just like the first paragraph, include examples that will back up your claims.

Here is an example below:

> A destitute Rowling was determined to write the first Harry Potter book, but she suffered a lot through the entire process. She eventually got on welfare so her and her daughter could afford to eat and have a place to stay. Rowling once said that she and her daughter were "poor as it is possible to be in modern Britain, without being homeless" so welfare was the answer to their desperate needs (Wikipedia). Perhaps even her economical situation played a large role in the Weasley's monetary troubles in the Harry Potter series. Despite having very little, Rowling mapped out and finished the first book. Her next mission was to get it published, but that was another arduous journey for her as well.

Body Paragraph #3: Rejection After Rejection

The third theme, rejection, is portrayed in this paragraph. Like the other two, we are expounding on how and why Rowling's early writing career was influenced by her persona life.

Here is an example below:

> As if Rowling hadn't already faced enough trials in her life, getting the Harry Potter manuscript published was another blow. Twelve different publishing houses rejected the manuscript, but that didn't deter Rowling

from succeeding. She used every rejection as motivation to send it to the next publisher. In the series, the main character Harry Potter is countlessly rejected from his Aunt Petunia, Uncle Vernon, and Cousin Dudley, which Rowling infused from her own life. This was just another situation that played a vital theme in the Harry Potter series.

Body Paragraph #4: The Triumph of Harry Potter

Last but not least, the last theme we are discussing in the research paper is the theme of triumph. This paragraph, in chronological order, wraps up all the other themes, which lead up to this one.

Here is an example below:

> Perhaps the most well-known (and inspiring) theme in the Harry Potter series is triumph. At the end of each novel, Harry Potter overcomes evil and experiences triumph with his friends and loved ones. Although Rowling experienced much tribulation, she overcame it in the end and grew immensely wealthy and famous from it. The theme of triumph weaves in and out of the series to show readers (just like Rowling's life) that overcoming obstacles is always possible despite how dim the situation is. Rowling's writing career is a testament to that.

The Conclusion

After completing the body paragraphs with solid evidence to back up your thesis, the conclusion nicely sums up the entire paper and gives a recap of the thesis. Writing the conclusion shouldn't be too difficult since you've already written the rest of the research paper.

Here is an example below:

> The themes of loss, abandonment, and rejection all play a vital role in the Harry Potter series, as well as Rowling's early writing career. Had she

not experienced those troubling times, perhaps the famous series would not be the same. Overall, Rowling used her tragic experiences both metaphorically and physically to inspire hope in not only readers but also people who are going through those same situations.

After completing each section, here is an example of the rough draft in its entirety:

Becoming a literary icon usually happens in an author's posthumous life. For J.K. Rowling, it happened almost overnight. After selling more than 400 million copies of the Harry Potter books and having the second largest grossing film series, Rowling quickly became the one of the most beloved children's author of all time. However, the authoress faced a series of devastating trials while writing the early beginnings of the magical world. With the success of the Harry Potter series and her own "rags to riches" story, J.K. Rowling's writing career portrays a triumph of poverty, manuscript rejections, and tragic losses in her life.

When the inception of Harry Potter occurred, Rowling experienced loss and abandonment in her life, which eventually played a vital role in the main character's life. The first tragic loss was Rowling's mother. She passed away right before Rowling told her about a new book idea she conjured. Soon after, Rowling experienced a heightened sense of abandonment. Her husband left and divorced her, leaving Rowling and her young daughter penniless. However, Rowling kept outlining and sketching out the early works of the Harry Potter series, infusing personal life experiences into some of the most beloved characters of all time.

A destitute Rowling was determined to write the first Harry Potter book, but she suffered a lot through the entire process. She eventually got on welfare so her and her daughter could afford to eat and have a place to stay. Rowling once said that she and her daughter were "poor as it is possible to be in modern Britain, without being homeless" so welfare was the answer to their desperate needs (Wikipedia). Perhaps even her economical situation played a large role in the Weasley's monetary troubles in the Harry Potter series. Despite having very little, Rowling mapped out and finished the first book. Her next mission was to get it published, but that was another arduous journey for her as well.

As if Rowling hadn't already faced enough trials in her life, getting the Harry Potter manuscript published was another blow. Twelve different publishing houses rejected the manuscript, but that didn't deter Rowling from succeeding. She used every rejection as motivation to send it to the next publisher. In the series, the main character Harry Potter is countlessly rejected from his Aunt Petunia, Uncle Vernon, and Cousin Dudley, which Rowling infused from her own life. This was just another situation that played a vital theme in the Harry Potter series.

Perhaps the most well-known (and inspiring) theme in the Harry Potter series is triumph. At the end of each novel, Harry Potter overcomes evil and experiences triumph with his friends and loved ones. Although Rowling experienced much tribulation, she overcame it in the end and grew immensely wealthy and famous from it. The theme of triumph weaves in and out of the series to show readers (just like Rowling's life) that overcoming obstacles is always possible despite how dim the situation is. Rowling's writing career is a testament to that

The themes of loss, abandonment, and rejection all play a vital role in the Harry Potter series, as well as Rowling's early writing career. Had she not experienced those troubling times, perhaps the famous series would not be the same. Overall, Rowling used her tragic experiences both metaphorically and physically to inspire hope in not only readers but also people who are going through those same situations.

Conclusion

Congrats! You finished your rough draft (which isn't an easy feat). After working through and finishing each section, hopefully your rough draft looks almost complete. Whether you're the type of writer that likes to power through and finish it in one sitting, or take your time to work on each part by itself, your rough draft will take a great amount of time, focus and motivation. Hopefully this chapter inspired you to write the best rough draft possible and feel inspired to start working on your own.

Although you just completed your rough draft, put it away for a day or two, then get ready for the revision process. It will take patience and time to make it perfect. Let's start editing!

"In writing, you must kill all your darlings."

- WILLIAM FAULKNER

CHAPTER 27

Becoming Your Worst Critic (The Revision Process)

Revising your rough draft is a tedious process to go through, but it will make your research paper better in the end. Apart from preparing and writing your rough draft, the revision process is the most important step when completing your final draft. Even if you write a terrible rough draft, revising your work thoroughly will make your final draft great, no matter what. Take your time working through this chapter, and re-work some of the steps if needed. Editing your research paper takes a great amount of time, so give yourself an ample amount to revise any grammar errors, organizational mistakes, thesis re-writes and more.

This chapter will help you understand what the revision process is and why it's needed, go through the five steps of revision and memorize essential rules to the editing process. You're going to be tired, frustrated and want to give up, but it'll be worth it in the end when you receive an excellent grade on your paper. Let's begin the revision process, shall we?

What is a revision process, and why is it needed?

A ***revision process*** consists of editing and re-editing your rough draft until the final draft version is complete. This step in the writing process takes much time to complete. By the end of revising your research paper, it probably won't look anything like your original draft – and that's the whole purpose of this process.

Revising your rough draft is like putting the finishing touches on your final work. Your first draft is just a more filled-out skeleton of the final version. You finally have words to work with and make into an excellent research paper. It takes more than just improving grammar or deleting sentences. Revising includes revamping evidence, the flow of your research paper, and even how your paragraphs are organized. Taking your time to edit your research paper will help in you in the end.

Below are the five steps in revising your research paper. If you need to go back and rework any of the steps or need to spend a long time on one, then go ahead and do it. Make sure you spend an adequate amount of time making sure your rough drafts keep getting better and better.

Five Steps of Revising Your Research Paper

Each step will help you rework your rough draft. The amount of time you will spend on each step will vary. Remember: these steps are here to make your research paper better in the end, so take your help and use this chapter as a helpful resource for editing your work.

Step 1: Find your main point, and refocus if needed

This is a basic yet essential step in revising your rough draft. Sometimes when you're writing a research paper, getting off topic can happen very easily. So the first step is to identify what your intended main point was and determine if you executed that in your rough draft.

First, let's re-read the introduction to identify if our intended main topic appears in the paper:

> Becoming a literary icon usually happens in an author's posthumous life. For J.K. Rowling, it happened almost overnight. After selling more than 400 million copies of the Harry Potter books and having the second largest grossing film series, Rowling quickly became the one of the most beloved children's author of all time. However, the authoress faced a series of devastating trials while writing the early beginnings of the magical world. With the success of the Harry Potter series and her own "rags to riches" story, J.K. Rowling's writing career portrays a triumph of poverty, manuscript rejections, and tragic losses in her life.

For our research paper on J.K. Rowling's writing career, we changed our early topic from focusing on her entire life and writing (which was included in our outline) to just focusing on her writing career.

Next, we refined our main topic even further and focused on her rise to literary fame with the Harry Potter series. In our introduction, we could make our introduction better if we focused more on how Harry Potter helped her rise to literary fame:

> Rising to literary fame usually happens posthumously for authors. For J.K. Rowling, it happened almost overnight when the Harry Potter series was published. After selling more than 400 million books and having the second largest grossing film series, Rowling quickly became the one of the most beloved children's author of all time. However, the authoress faced a series of devastating trials while writing the early beginnings of

the magical world. With the success of the Harry Potter series and her own "rags to riches" story, J.K. Rowling's writing career portrays a triumph of poverty, manuscript rejections, and tragic losses in her life.

The introduction is more succinct and helps the reader understand what the main topic is before even reading the rest of the research paper. Now let's move on to reevaluating your paper's audience.

Step 2: Reevaluate your audience

The second step is reevaluating your audience. Determining who your reader is will set the tone, style, and layout of your research paper. For instance, scientific research papers will have a serious tone, backed up by a plethora of evidence. For English research papers, the tone can be more flowery, flowing, and written with different types of resources.

For our research paper's audience, we have the option to write with more fluidity and flowery language:

> Rising to literary fame usually happens posthumously for authors. For J.K. Rowling, it happened almost overnight when the Harry Potter series was published. After selling more than 400 million books and having the second largest grossing film series, Rowling quickly became the one of the most beloved children's author of all time. However, the authoress faced a series of devastating trials while writing the early beginnings of the magical world. With the success of the Harry Potter series and her own "rags to riches" story, J.K. Rowling's writing career portrays a triumph of poverty, manuscript rejections, and tragic losses in her life.

Let's make this introduction's language more intriguing while presenting the thesis and the paper's evidence:

> Rising to literary fame typically happens posthumously for authors. For J.K. Rowling, becoming a beloved children's author almost overnight.

> After selling more than 400 million books and having the second largest grossing film series, Rowling quickly rose to stardom when the Harry Potter series was published. However, the authoress faced a series of devastating trials while writing the early beginnings of the magical world. With the success of the Harry Potter series and her own "rags to riches" story, J.K. Rowling's writing career portrays a triumph of poverty, manuscript rejections, and tragic losses in her life.

This edit not only livens up the language of the research paper but also makes the thesis and argument more compelling.

Step 3: Eliminate excess paragraphs and wordiness

The next step in the revision process is eliminating all unnecessary wordiness. This will probably give you the most trouble when editing your research paper. You've stared at your own work for so long that it's difficult to discover any excessive language, but this is a vital step in editing your work. Once you've practiced looking for different and better ways to rework your paper, then you'll truly become a writing (and editing) master.

Let's look at our introduction below:

> Rising to literary fame typically happens posthumously for authors. For J.K. Rowling, becoming a beloved children's author happened almost overnight. After selling more than 400 million books and having the second largest grossing film series, Rowling quickly rose to stardom when the Harry Potter series was published. However, the authoress faced a series of devastating trials while writing the early beginnings of the magical world. With the success of the Harry Potter series and her own "rags to riches" story, J.K. Rowling's writing career portrays a triumph of poverty, manuscript rejections, and tragic losses in her life.

Although this introduction has come a long way since the rough draft, there is still quite a bit of wordiness that we can eliminate. So let's eliminate our excessive use of words:

> Rising to literary fame ~~typically happens~~ posthumously for authors. For J.K. Rowling, becoming a beloved children's author occurred almost overnight. After selling more than 400 million books ~~and having the second largest grossing film series~~, Rowling quickly rose to stardom when the Harry Potter series was published. However, the authoress faced a series of devastating trials while writing ~~the early beginnings of the magical world. With the success of the Harry Potter series and~~ her own "rags to riches" story, J.K. Rowling's writing career portrays a triumph of poverty, manuscript rejections, and tragic losses in her life.

As you can see, we deleted some of the language that we didn't need in the introduction. It's always best to "kill your little darlings" even if you think your writing looks fine. Let's move on to the next step.

Step 4: Check for grammar and any other errors

For this step, editing your research paper also includes checking for grammar and other errors. This means you can incorporate all the tricks you learned in the previous grammar chapters on your research paper. Check for any misspellings, dangling modifiers, incorrect usage of words and other grammar issues.

Let's identify any grammar errors in the introduction:

> Rising to literary fame occurs posthumously for authors. For J.K. Rowling, becoming a beloved children's author occurred almost overnight. After selling more than 400 million books, Rowling quickly rose to stardom when the Harry Potter series was published. However, the authoress faced a series of devastating trials while writing. In her own "rags to riches" story,

J.K. Rowling's writing career portrays a triumph of poverty, manuscript rejections, and tragic losses in her life.

We can tighten up the language more and make it even more succinct:

Rising to literary fame typically occurs in an author's posthumous life. For J.K. Rowling, becoming a beloved children's author happened during the beginning of her writing career. After selling more than 400 million books, Rowling rose to fame when the Harry Potter series was published and met with wild success. Despite her immense success, the authoress faced a series of devastating trials while writing the book series. J.K. Rowling portrays her "rags to riches" writing career through a triumph over poverty, manuscript rejections, and tragic losses in the Harry Potter series.

After reworking some of the language, our introduction reads and flows much better than before. Make sure you find all the grammar mistakes in your research paper when you edit it.

Step 5: Repeat all steps if needed

This step is just a reminder to work on any aspect in particular. Not sure if your main topic is clear enough? Go back and rework it. Want to make your introduction less wordy? Then re-read it and eliminate all wordiness. Take your time making sure you've edited everything in your research paper before moving on to another step.

Rules to Remember When Editing Your Rough Draft

When you're done working through each step, here are some rules to remember when you're editing your rough draft. These rules will motivate and encourage you to edit your work thoroughly, no matter how arduous the process is.

Rule #1: The editing process takes more than one revision.

Yes, this rule is too true. Although this chapter only did one revision of just the introduction, your entire research paper will need to be edited at least two or three times. The more revisions that you take the time to do, the more high quality your research paper will be. It's some great to keep in mind.

Rule #2: Take your time and be patient when editing your rough draft.

Don't rush through editing your work! It won't help you in the end. Give yourself an entire day to look over your work. As for the second and third revision, put your paper away for a few days to give yourself a break. If you edit your work in small doses, then it'll be more beneficial for you and your research paper in the end.

Conclusion

You made it through the tedious revision process – hooray! After analyzing every sentence, paragraph, and idea, your research paper is probably looking amazing. With the help of methodical steps and easy-to-remember rules, the revision process isn't as bad as it seems. If you give yourself enough time to work on your research paper, then this process won't be as stressful or bothersome.

Critiquing your own work isn't easy (and it definitely takes a prolific writer to be objective to his or her own writing), but it's definitely a skill that you'll not only need but also can learn with tons of practice. After making it through each long revision, let's move one step closer to the finish line: rewriting your research paper.

> "The most valuable of all talents is that of never using two words when one will do."
>
> **- THOMAS JEFFERSON**

CHAPTER 28

Write, Write, and Rewrite

Even though you probably feel like you've reworked your research paper enough and that it's most likely perfect, the best writers will rewrite their work more than once or twice. Just like the revision process, you may feel tired and frustrated while working through it. But once you make it to the other side, all your hard work will pay off. Rewriting takes time and perseverance, but you will become a great writer once you practice doing this step. All talented writers write and rewrite until their fingers are sore; and you're no different!

This chapter will help you understand what the rewriting process looks like, answer common questions about rewriting a work, and go over some do's and don'ts of rewriting your research paper. As stated, the more time you allow yourself to work on this step, the less stressed you'll be when reworking each section. Let's get started!

What does the rewriting process look like?

The ***rewriting process*** consists of rewriting your paper's introduction, body paragraphs, and conclusion. As mentioned, it's best to rewrite your research paper at least two or three times. The more you rewrite any part of your paper, the better it will be.

Rewriting your work doesn't necessarily mean you'll discard your first rough draft and rewrite the entire content again. (That would be quite fruitless.) You don't need to do that, but you may need to rewrite a paragraph or two. It's tough conveying your main points and thesis on the first time. Writers get bogged down with writing a great amount of words, so they lose focus and creativity to portray their evidential points.

Common Questions About Rewriting

Below are some common questions about rewriting your paper. Hopefully these questions will help you understand why rewriting is essential for moving closer to your final draft.

"Why should I keep re-writing?"

Unfortunately, this is a very common question. Most writers think their rough draft should be there final draft, but this isn't the case at all. Whether you're a beginning writer or a famous author, it will always take more than one draft to write the best paper possible.

Take a look at the first draft of a body paragraph then the final draft after going through various edits:

> When the inception of Harry Potter occurred, Rowling experienced loss and abandonment in her life, which eventually played a vital role in the main character's life. The first tragic loss was Rowling's mother. She passed away right before Rowling told her about a new book idea she conjured. Soon after, Rowling experienced a heightened sense of abandonment. Her husband left and divorced her, leaving Rowling and her young daughter penniless. However, Rowling kept outlining and sketching out the early works of the Harry Potter series, infusing personal life experiences into some of the most beloved characters of all time.

When Rowling started outlining the world of Harry Potter, Rowling experienced loss and abandonment in her life. This eventually played a vital role in the background story of Harry Potter. The first tragic loss Rowling experienced was losing her mother. She passed away right before Rowling had the chance to tell her about her new book idea. This was just one blow to Rowling's detrimental life. Rowling soon experienced abandonment. After a few years of marriage, her husband divorced her, leaving Rowling and her young daughter penniless and fending for themselves. Despite these conditions, Rowling kept outlining the early works of the Harry Potter series for 5 years, infusing her own life experiences into some of the most beloved – and relatable – characters of all time.

Do you see the difference in the two paragraphs? The latter one elaborates on Rowling's personal tragedies and makes it flow better. This is just one example why rewriting truly improves your writing.

"How many times should I keep rewriting?"

This answer depends on your original rough draft and editing process. Typically, you'll still need to rewrite your work two or three more times, but sometimes you'll do less or more rewrites. So, it'll depend on a case-to-case basis.

As for rewriting our research paper on J.K. Rowling's writing career, we rewrote the research paper twice after we checked for grammar, sentence clarity, organizational flow, and strong evidential points. Once you've checked everything, then you'll be done rewriting your research paper.

"When will I know the rewriting process is done?"

The answer is the same for the last question. Once you've rewritten everything that needed work, then you'll be done. However, with that being said, you'll still need to take your time determining whether you're done or not.

Do's and Don'ts of The Rewriting Process

Below are some "do's and don'ts" to keep in mind when rewriting your research paper. These tips will help you succeed in the writing process. Remember to use these tips as reference as you rewrite.

Don't overwrite.

Yes, this can happen very easily, especially for beginning writers. When rewriting your research paper, make sure you're only reworking parts of your rough draft that need work; don't make extra work for yourself. So when you rewrite a section, put it away for a day or two, then come back to it. You'll have fresh eyes and see if it still needs more work or not.

Take a break from the rewriting process.

Step away from your writing every once in awhile. Overworking yourself won't help your writing at all. First, don't pressure yourself to get your writing done in a short amount of time. Give yourself plenty of time, and make sure you're focusing on the quality of your writing. Once you've reworked a section, either work on another section or take a break. This will help your writing overall.

Know when to stop.

Sometimes, writers can rework their writing too much. There is a balance to rewriting your work and knowing when the paper has reached its limit. If you bog yourself down with rewrite after rewrite, then this step's purpose will be defeated. As you work through your paper, you'll know when to stop. Your paper will flow, you won't see any writing errors, and your evidence will support your thesis. It won't take 10 rewrites to get to this point, too.

Conclusion

You're probably tired of rewriting your research paper, but take a second to compare your rough draft to your rewritten drafts. Do you see any signs of improvement? If you've reworked your paper enough, then your current draft should look nothing like your first one. That's the point of this chapter. Typically, any first draft is going to need work (even the great writers say that), and that's totally acceptable. As long as you analyze each section, and even down to each sentence, then your final draft will be impeccable.

After finishing this chapter, you're almost close to the finish line. But first, it's good to give your eyes a break and let someone else look at your work. Let's move on to the next chapter: the peer review stage.

CHAPTER 29
Peer Review

Having a peer (which can be another student or even an adult) edit your work always benefits your writing. No matter how many times you re-read your work, you are bound to miss a mistake or miss out on rearranging ideas or sections in a better order. Listening and accepting peer critiques can be very difficult for some writers. Seeing more critiques on a paper they've worked so hard on can be discouraging. However, accepting peer review mark-ups and being open to new ideas will benefit your paper overall.

This chapter will help you understand what a peer review is, ask whether you need a peer review on your rough draft, and have some rules to keep in mind when going through the peer review process. Hopefully, this step isn't too time-consuming, and you can get some great advice and critiques to improve your research paper.

What is a peer review?

A *peer review* is when you have someone edit or give feedback on your writing, whether in its entirety or on a section or two. Peer review can come in different forms, such as having someone edit your research paper with a red pen, reading over the work and giving feedback (i.e. tips, advice), or a combination of both. Having someone look over your work is extremely beneficial to you. There are going to be some errors in your writing that you might overlook, and having someone edit your paper will catch it for you.

If you want a thorough peer review, then have two or three peers or adults look over your work. Typically, each reviewer will catch something in your writing that you or another person might not catch. This step usually doesn't take too much time because your draft should pretty much resemble the final draft.

Questions to Consider

Here are some questions to consider when using peers as editors. Ask yourself these questions before beginning the peer review process. Keep in mind that this step's purpose is to make you a better writer, not feeling dejected from constructive criticism.

Should I have a peer review my rough draft?

The answer should almost always be yes. As mentioned, peer reviewers make your writing better overall. They can give constructive or encouraging feedback, point out grammar or writing errors you may struggle with, and let you know how the paper reads in its entirety. Find a peer or adult who is a great writer because they are guaranteed to make you a better writer, too.

Do I really need feedback?

Yes, receiving and listening to feedback really helps improve your writing. Although it's hard to swallow critiques and other edits to your research paper (which you've worked so hard on), the edits and advice will help you in the end. The point of this step is to get you one step closer to perfecting your final draft, so use their feedback as a resourceful tool for revamping your research paper.

Rules to Keep In Mind When Having A Peer Review Your Work

After understanding why the peer review step is so vital to revising your research paper, here are some rules to keep in mind when you're having peers critique your work:

1. Choose a good peer reviewer

Although you might think anybody would make a good peer reviewer, this isn't always the case. Make sure you pick a student, teacher, or adult who will give reliable, honest feedback on your research paper. The more proficient the peer reviewer is, the more useful his or her feedback will be. If you choose a bad peer reviewer, listen to his or her feedback, and incorporate it into your research paper, then your writing will suffer immensely. Take your time picking an excellent peer reviewer,

2. Understand the peer reviewer's comments and edits

Once the peer reviewer has edited and read over your work, sit down with him or her to go over the feedback. Ask him or her to explain why they made certain edits and what else the research paper needs overall. Maybe you'll need to explain your argument more, add more depth to your thesis, or simply make the organizational flow better. Whatever it is, make sure you understand your errors and how to correct them for the final draft.

3. Deal with constructive criticism well

Once the peer reviewer has explained his or edits and feedback, use the constructive criticism for your research paper's benefit. Don't get discouraged if your paper is marked up with tons of red. This will help you write a great final draft. Beginning writers struggle to see peer review edits in a positive way, but they really do help your writing in the end.

4. Not all edits and comments should factor into your work.

You're probably confused by this rule, but it's actually the best one to keep in mind. Even though you've picked the best peers or adults to review your work, you shouldn't always factor their edits into your work. You should always, however, consider their feedback and edits in an objective light, but sometimes you don't need to incorporate them into your work. Just make sure that their edits and feedback are benefitting you and your research paper in the end.

Example

Here is an example below of receiving and using peer-review feedback:

A destitute Rowling was determined to write the first Harry Potter book, but she suffered a lot through the entire process. She eventually got on welfare so her and her daughter could afford to eat and have a place to stay. Rowling once said that she and her daughter were "poor as it is possible to be in modern Britain, without being homeless" so welfare was the answer to their desperate needs (Wikipedia). Perhaps even her economical situation played a large role in the Weasley's monetary troubles in the Harry Potter series. Despite having very little, Rowling mapped out and finished the first book. Her next mission was to get it published, but that was another arduous journey for her as well.

If we had a peer look over this section and give feedback, they might give us the following edits and suggestions:

"I love the piece of evidence you used in this section. However, I suggest rearranging your evidence and the entire flow of this paragraph. You may also want to consider including more references to back up your claim."

After taking this feedback into account, here is what our revised paragraph looks like:

> Even though Rowling was destitute and depressed, she wrote and finished the first Harry Potter book. Still, she suffered a lot through the entire process. Rowling eventually signed up for welfare so she and her daughter didn't live in poor conditions anymore (Thomas, 144). The authoress once said that she and her daughter were "poor as it is possible to be in modern Britain, without being homeless," so welfare was the answer to their desperate needs (Wikipedia, 13). If Rowling had never experienced poverty at such a critical level, then perhaps her economical situation would have never played a large role in the Harry Potter series, as portrayed in the Weasley's monetary troubles. Despite having very little means, Rowling created an entire magical world where anything is possible.

Without peer review feedback, this paragraph would not have been revised as well as it was after taking each tip into consideration. The purpose of peer review is to make your writing the best that it can be.

Conclusion

After viewing some examples and understanding how peer review can boost your research paper, hopefully this process has helped you take one step further to completing your final draft. Between rewriting your paper and having others give you feedback and advice, your research paper is on its way to being finished. Yes, it's a very long, arduous process, but it's indeed necessary. If you can find a friend who is a great writer, or know an adult who writes extremely well, then you should run your research paper through the peer review process.

Now, you've completed all the steps that lead up to the final draft. Before you move on to the last chapter and finalize your final draft, make sure you've fully completed each former chapter and step. If you need to go back, then, by all means, go back through it. If you feel confident in your research paper, then head on over to the last chapter: the final draft.

"I love deadlines. I love the whooshing noise they make as they go by."

- DOUGLAS ADAMS

CHAPTER 30
The Final Draft

It's the moment you've been waiting for. After working tirelessly on each former step, writing the final draft is the finishing touch to all the hard work you've put into your research paper. Before you send in or print your research paper, it's important to double-check your work. From the title sheet to grammar to the bibliography section, the final draft consists of making sure everything is correct and nothing is missing.

This chapter will help you understand what the final draft consists of, introduce you to the final draft checklist and take you through the entire final editing process.

The *final draft* is the final product of your research paper. After brainstorming your topic, outlining your draft, researching resources, writing numerous rough drafts, editing your paper, and rewriting different sections, your final draft is the finishing touch of all your labor. This last step is essentially a quick checklist to see if you need to change anything.

Below is the checklist you should refer to when finishing your final draft. As always, make sure you take your time when completing this step. All your fruits of labor will pay off when you receive a high score and are commended by your teacher! Let's begin.

The Final Draft Checklist

Using the final draft checklist will help you go over your final draft and make sure that you didn't miss out on anything. For example, you might have forgotten to print out your title page, or to include a bibliography at the end of your research paper. Running through each part of your final draft will perfect your research paper.

1. The Grammar Aspect

Although you've looked over grammar during the editing, rewriting and peer revision stages, checking for grammar one more time is always a good idea. There might be a period you forgot to include, or a word is misspelled in your title. Either way, scan your final draft for any grammar errors. You'll be upset with yourself if you turn in your research paper and you spelled a simple word wrong.

Grammar Mistakes

Grammar mistakes can include any of the following but aren't limited to: misspelled words, run-on-sentences, dangling modifiers, use of too many adverbs, wordiness, capitalization, passive voice, transitional devices, sentence clarity, and more. Take your time working through each sentence and making sure you've caught every mistake.

2. Structural Aspect

As stated, you've already checked over the structural aspect of your research paper many times, but it's always good to check one last time. Perhaps you might switch two paragraphs around or want to position your thesis in a different part of the introduction. Make sure you are objectively analyzing if your research paper's structure is exceptional for the final draft.

Introduction

Does your introduction set the tone for the rest of the research paper, or is it separate from following sections? Do you present your thesis and supportive evidence well, or should you rearrange the format? Did you use excellent grammar, sentence fluidity, succinct language, and organizational flow? Asking yourself these questions will help you identify any problems in the introduction.

Body

Do your body paragraphs support your thesis and other claims? Can the reader logically come to the same conclusion as your thesis does? Did you use great grammar, style, organizational flow, useful transitional devices, sentence clarity, and helpful evidence? Is there another better way to position your body paragraphs? These questions will help correct any writing, style or grammar issues in your body paragraphs.

Conclusion

Does your conclusion sum up the rest of your research paper without being redundant? Does your thesis and supportive arguments make sense? Do you need to rearrange their position in the conclusion? Are there any other ways to present your argument again? Did you write enough to wrap up the entire research paper? Your conclusion is the final thought, so make sure you've stated everything that you want included.

3. Technical Aspect

You should devote a great amount of time checking over the technical aspect of your final draft. Before now, you haven't been checking if the title page is correct, or if you included enough bibliographies at the end of the paper. Take your time checking if your research paper's title page, writing style format, headers, and bibliographies are all done correctly.

Title Page

Does your title page include your name, date, the paper's title, and the name of the course? Do you need to include your teacher's name, too? Is everything formatted correctly on a separate page? It may seem strange to thoroughly check over your title page, but you'd be surprised to see how many writers struggle with this aspect.

Styling

Have you formatted your entire research paper correctly? Did you remember to correctly attribute in different sections of the paper? Did you remember to include headings, references, and other stylistic formats? Make sure your paper's styling is correct; it's easy to mess up on this part.

Bibliography

Did you include a bibliography for every resource you used in the book? Is it properly placed at the end of your research paper? Is there anything else you need to improve or include? Check your bibliography page to make sure you didn't forget anything.

Questions to Ask Yourself

Here are some last-minute questions to ask yourself before you email or print out your final draft. It's always better to take your time and make sure you do the best job possible on your final draft.

"Did you include everything you needed and wanted to include?

This is always a great question to ask yourself. If you haven't included another resource, or elaborated on a certain piece of evidence, then make sure you add those in as soon as possible. Your final draft should have everything you want to have in it, so take your time and make sure everything is there.

"Does your research paper completely answer your assignment?"

By your final draft, it should be clear whether or not your research paper answers your writing assignment's prompt. If it doesn't then you need to go back a few steps and find out what went wrong. But typically, you'll have written an excellent final draft that properly answers your writing assignment, so no need to fret over this question.

Here is an example of our final draft:

> Rising to literary fame typically occurs in an author's posthumous life. For J.K. Rowling, becoming a beloved children's author happened during the beginning of her writing career. After selling more than 400 million books, Rowling rose to fame when the Harry Potter series was published and met with wild success. Despite her immense success, the authoress faced a series of devastating trials while writing the book series. J.K. Rowling portrays her "rags to riches" writing career through a triumph over poverty, manuscript rejections, and tragic losses in the Harry Potter series.
>
> When Rowling started outlining the world of Harry Potter, Rowling experienced loss and abandonment in her life. This eventually played a vital

role in the background story of Harry Potter. The first tragic loss Rowling experienced was losing her mother. She passed away right before Rowling had the chance to tell her about her new book idea. This was just one blow to Rowling's detrimental life. Rowling soon experienced abandonment. After a few years of marriage, her husband divorced her, leaving Rowling and her young daughter penniless and fending for themselves. Despite these conditions, Rowling kept outlining the early works of the Harry Potter series for 5 years, infusing her own life experiences into some of the most beloved – and relatable – characters of all time.

Even though Rowling was destitute and depressed, she wrote and finished the first Harry Potter book. Still, she suffered a lot through the entire process. Rowling eventually signed up for welfare so she and her daughter didn't live in poor conditions anymore (Thomas, 144). The authoress once said that she and her daughter were "poor as it is possible to be in modern Britain, without being homeless," so welfare was the answer to their desperate needs (Wikipedia, 13). If Rowling had never experienced poverty at such a critical level, then perhaps her economical situation would have never played a large role in the Harry Potter series, as portrayed in the Weasley's monetary troubles. Despite having very little means, Rowling created an entire magical world where anything is possible.

As if Rowling hadn't already faced enough trials in her life, publishing the Harry Potter manuscript was another obstacle to overcome. Twelve different publishing houses rejected the manuscript, but that didn't deter Rowling from succeeding. She used every rejection as motivation to send it to the next publisher. In the series, the main character Harry Potter is countlessly rejected from his Aunt Petunia, Uncle Vernon, and Cousin Dudley, which Rowling infused from her own life. This was just another situation that played a vital theme in the Harry Potter series.

Perhaps the most well known (and inspiring) theme in the Harry Potter series is triumph. At the end of each novel, Harry Potter overcomes evil and experiences triumph with his friends and loved ones. Although Rowling experienced much tribulation, she overcame it in the end and grew immensely wealthy and famous from it. The theme of triumph weaves in and out of the series to show readers (just like Rowling's life) that overcoming obstacles is always possible despite how dim the situation is. Rowling's writing career is a testament to that

Loss, abandonment, and rejection are the main themes that play a vital role in the Harry Potter series, as well as Rowling's early writing career. Had she not experienced those troubling times, perhaps the famous series would not be the same. Overall, Rowling uses her tragic experiences to inspire hope in not only readers but also anyone who is going through those same situations.

After reworking each section a few times, we believe this final draft contains the best flow, organization, flawless grammar, strong thesis, and well-backed up evidence. Your research paper should exude the same – that's when you'll know your final draft is complete!

Congratulations – You did it!

After all your hard work, you're finally ready to turn your paper in. Congratulations! Once the entire process is done, you'll notice how each step was vital to writing a great research paper. Good writing takes great effort, but if you're patient enough to get through it, then you'll see amazing results.

Hopefully, Part 3 taught you a lot about the writing process and will challenge you to become the best writer you can be.

CONCLUSION

You probably feel like a grammar guru and writing professional by now. Hopefully each chapter and exercise proved beneficial for you and your writing endeavors. As long as you keep reading different materials (from newspapers to online articles to fun reads), writing, and reviewing your work, then you will become a great writer. Anything that is successful never comes without failure and commitment.

Writing is an ongoing process that will sometimes naturally become better, but most of the time it takes practice and determination. Even though you've finished this book, it's a good idea to go through it again and again just to refresh your mind about tricky grammar rules and how you can keep improving your writing. If you do this, then you will impress every college professor and excel in class.

As promised, the end of this guide contains answers to exercises, a glossary of terms that were discussed in each chapter, a list of action verbs that will strengthen your writing, and additional links to other resources. Use these well. These resources will help you so much whenever your struggle with grammar or writing.

And with that, this book comes to a close. Remember—good writing takes practice. Never give up if you lack in an area. If some of the great writers had given up, then the world would be a very different place. Great writing is attainable—even for you.

Good luck on your future writing endeavors!

ANSWERS TO EXERCISES

As promised, here are the answers to every exercise provided in each chapter. If you struggle with getting the answers correct, then keep re-practicing each exercise until you understand why the given answer is correct.

Chapter 1. What is Grammar?

A. Your and You're (p 17)

A-1 your	**A-3** you're	**A-5** your
A-2 you're	**A-4** you're	

B. There, Their, and They're (p 19)

B-1 their	**B-3** there	**B-5** their
B-2 they're	**B-4** there	**B-6** they're

C. Pronoun-Antecedent Errors (p 21)

C-1 is	**C-3** is
C-2 its	**C-4** its

D. Run-on Sentences (Or Comma Splices) (p 23)

D-1 correct	**D-3** incorrect
D-2 incorrect	**D-4** correct

E. It's and Its (p 24)

E-1	correct	**E-3**	correct	**E-5**	incorrect
E-2	incorrect	**E-4**	correct		

F. Whom vs. Who (p 26)

F-1	whom	**F-3**	who
F-2	who	**F-4**	whom

Chapter 2. Spelling/Capitalization

A. Accept and Except (p 33)

A-1	accept	**A-3**	except	**A-5**	except
A-2	accept	**A-4**	accept		

B. Affect and Effect (p 34)

B-1	effect	**B-3**	affect
B-2	affect	**B-4**	effect

C. We're, Were, and Where (p 36)

C-1	where	**C-3**	were	**C-5**	where
C-2	we're	**C-4**	were	**C-6**	we're

D. To, Two, and Too (p 37)

D-1	two	**D-3**	to	**D-5**	too
D-2	too	**D-4**	to	**D-6**	two

E. Advice and Advise (p 38)

E-1	advice	**E-3**	advise
E-2	advise	**E-4**	advice

F. Then and Than (p 39)

F-1	than	**F-3**	then
F-2	then	**F-4**	than

G. Led and Lead (p 40)

G-1 led

G-3 lead

G-2 lead

G-4 led

H. Conscious and Conscience (p 41)

H-1 conscious

H-3 conscious

H-2 conscience

H-4 conscience

I. Capitalization (p 47)

I-1 <u>O</u>n the 8th day, our dog <u>P</u>enny found her way back home after being lost!

I-2 When will <u>S</u>esame <u>S</u>treet be on TV again?

I-3 Beneath the bridge were two cats named <u>P</u>atty and <u>M</u>addy.

I-4 Although <u>D</u>enise lives on <u>H</u>ampton <u>A</u>venue, I still visit her a lot.

I-5 <u>O</u>ther than that, Kevin is a pretty awesome kid.

I-6 <u>T</u>ommy didn't enjoy his birthday for some reason.

I-7 Can you take me to <u>M</u>ount <u>R</u>ushmore one day soon?

I-8 Please take <u>M</u>atilda to the nurse's office.

I-9 <u>D</u>id you see who climbed <u>M</u>ount <u>E</u>verest the other day?

I-10 Where can I take my little sister <u>J</u>amie to play outside?

Chapter 3. Adjectives & Adverbs

A. Adjectives (p 50)

A-1 orange, striped, running

A-3 scientific, hard, exhaustive

A-2 bright, ridiculous, horrible

A-4 tough, excellent, great

B. Adverbs (p 52)

B-1 fairly

B-3 cleverly

B-5 regularly

B-2 clearly

B-4 highly

Chapter 4. Articles & Appositives

A. A or An (p 56)

A-1 an

A-3 a

A-2 a

A-4 an

B. Articles (p 57)

B-1 the   **B-3** a   **B-5** the
B-2 a   **B-4** the

C. Appositives (p 58)

C-1 Wendy, **the fastest girl on the track team,** made sure that everyone saw her finish first during the race.

C-2 **Known for his wit,** Andrew became the valedictorian by a landslide.

C-3 Do you know Allie, **the prettiest girl in high school**?

C-4 Mr. Richards, **the oldest teacher at school,** had enough of the boy's shenanigans in class.

C-5 Can you believe Tiffany, **the nerdy girl,** was asked out by Timmy?

Chapter 5. Nouns and Pronouns

A. Nouns (p 63)

A-1 Can you tell me where exactly the men's **restroom** is?

A-2 Ben's research **report** went mysteriously missing today after **lunch**.

A-3 The **car** that we took to the **beach** broke down in the way **home**.

A-4 Are there any more **peaches** in the **kitchen**?

A-5 Although the **pie** was delicious, I didn't care for the mysterious meal's **ingredients**.

A-6 Oliver's **papers** went flying everywhere in the **classroom** today.

A-7 Quick and silent, the rats' **feet** scurried along the **floor**.

A-8 Did you decide whether **Lola** or **Peter** is coming to **dinner** tonight?

A-9 You have exquisite taste, **Mrs. Childers**; I love your couch's **fabric**!

A-10 The school director's **notebook** went missing today, and he seems furious.

B. Pronouns (p 65)

B-1 Is **anybody** willing to decorate the auditorium for the school play **this** weekend?

B-2 **I,** Denise, don't think **you** should do that because **you'll** get in trouble.

B-3 Hillary, **who** is the new girl, got a perfect score on **her** U.S. history exam.

B-4 **Someone** came earlier and dropped off a note for **you.**

B-5 Are **these** baseball pants **yours** or **mine**?

B-6 Walter, **whose** mom is very strict, was grounded for three months straight.

B-7 It's always best to treat others as **you'd** want to be treated.

B-8 Until **those** clothes are cleaned, **I** can't leave the house.

B-9 Xavier is **someone who** is always there for **you** when **you** need **him**.

B-10 I love **this** university; I feel like **anybody** could fit in here!

Chapter 6. Numbers

A. Numbers Rule 1 (p 68)

A-1 **One hundred and eighty** high school boys tried out for the football team this year.

A-2 **Twenty** little girls pranced onto the stage and started doing their practiced dance routine.

A-3 **Ninety-four** people waited in line for the new phone to come out the next day.

A-4 **Thirteen** cars were haphazardly parked all over the place.

A-5 **Twenty-five** percent of the cross-country team is freshmen.

A-6 **Forty-five** moms helped run the fall festival fundraiser this year.

A-7 **Twenty-one** puppies are for sale at the local animal shelter!

A-8 **Three hundred** seniors are going to graduate from Thomas Jefferson High School this year.

A-9 **Eight** new teachers were hired over the summer.

A-10 **Thirty-three** people now live in this neighborhood.

B. Numbers Rule 2 (p 71)

B-1 **Sixty-two** percent of girls in this high school have ambitions for getting into Ivy League schools.

B-2 **Twenty-one** eggs were used for this recipe.

B-3 **Forty-six** championship awards are polished weekly in the awards room.

B-4 **Eighty-eight** families have donated to this school over the years.

B-5 **Fifty-two** little leaguers stormed onto the field after the tournament was over.

B-6 **Thirty-seven** flower arrangements were ordered this morning!

B-7 **Forty-three** students were added to the 2017 freshmen class.

B-8 **Seventy-eight** percent of the students passed the history exam.

B-9 **Ninety-two** authors were born and raised in this state.

B-10 **Twenty-three** teachers are up for public school award nominations.

C. Numbers Rule 3 (p 73)

C-1 In **1969**, my father was born in Indianapolis.

C-2 Email and the Internet took over the business world in the early **2000's**.

C-3 In the late **1700's**, Jane Austen wrote the some of the best novels in the English language.

C-4 Did you know that America was very prosperous in the **1800's**?

C-5 In the **1900's**, industrialization soon took over the economy.

D. Numbers Rule 4 (p 75)

D-1 The Cold War erupted in the **'50s** and caused the United States and the USSR to have conflict.

D-2 The Roaring **'20s** was a time of excessive drinking, dancing, and frivolous fun.

D-3 In the **'90s**, the Internet was invented and started becoming useful for businesses.

D-4 Did you know that America's economy was pretty good in the **'40s**?

D-5 Please re-do your hair; you look like you should stepped out of an **'80s** flick.

E. Numbers Rule 5 (p 76)

E-1 correct

E-2 incorrect

E-3 incorrect

E-4 correct

E-5 incorrect

F. Numbers Rule 6 (p 77)

F-1 I need a **two-thirds** cup of sugar for this cookie recipe.

F-2 The principal said that my skirt needs to be **three-fifths** of an inch past my knee.

F-3 About **one-third** of the basketball team flunked their math exam.

F-4 About **five-sixths** of the band is made up of girls.

F-5 Can you tell that only **one-fourth** of this room is filled up?

G. Numbers Rule 7 (p 78)

G-1 noon

G-2 midnight

G-3 noon

G-4 noon

G-5 midnight

H. Numbers Rule 8 (p 79)

H-1 Man, what I would do with **$1 million**!

H-2 Can you believe that Mark Zuckerberg is worth **$3 billion**?

H-3 That house must be worth at least **$8 million**.

I. Numbers Rule 9 (p 80)

I-1 correct   **I-2** incorrect   **I-3** correct

Chapter 7. Prepositions

A. Prepositions (p 84)

A-1 Rachael and her three younger siblings ran **along** the edge of the neighborhood.

A-2 Is there a way that you can work **through** this pile of laundry in the afternoon?

A-3 The homecoming queen was lost in the crowd **among** fans and students.

A-4 We love to make popsicles and go swimming **during** the summer.

A-5 I believe Gina lives **near** the farmer's market and duck pond in Richmond.

A-6 **From** the stage, the singer leapt into the enthusiastic crowd.

A-7 There is this beautiful path with wild flowers and blueberries **across** the field.

A-8 **With** extra sleep and medicine, Nora kicked her cold and is feeling much better.

A-9 **If** you keep going left and past the cemetery, you'll find Ben's house.

A-10 Even though we had limited light and supplies, we trudged **through** the thick trees and bushes.

Chapter 8. Verbs

A. Action Verbs (p 89)

A-1 Professor X, from the X-Men movies, **combats** with his arch-nemesis at the end of the series.

A-2 Suffering from insomnia, the student **slept** through her morning classes.

A-3 Janice **slapped** John in the face when he stood her up on their date.

A-4 He **angered** me when he said that my paper was lousy.

A-5 Whether or not it's right, Naomi **kissed** Dick in the parking lot after school.

B. Linking Verbs (p 90)

B-1 <u>During the winter in the northeast</u>, the weather **is** sometimes frigid and unbearable to locals and visitors.

B-2 I **felt** <u>like my English teacher didn't notice how much effort I put into my personal essay</u>.

B-3 It **has been** <u>a crazy day filled with washing the car, mowing the lawn, and paying the bills</u>.

B-4 <u>Whether it's true or not</u>, the pep band **sounds** <u>like it hasn't practiced in the off-season</u>.

B-5 <u>When the caterpillar breaks from its cocoon</u>, it **becomes** a magnificent butterfly.

Chapter 9. Irregular Verbs

A. Irregular Verbs (p 95)

A-1 sung	**A-5** laid	**A-8** eaten, eat
A-2 come	**A-6** become	**A-9** drawn
A-3 are	**A-7** drunk	**A-10** tear
A-4 felt		

Chapter 10. Subject-Verb Agreement

A. Subject-Verb Agreement (p 100)

A-1 plans	**A-5** is	**A-8** are
A-2 is	**A-6** sings	**A-9** is
A-3 is	**A-7** is	**A-10** are
A-4 is		

Chapter 11. The Sentence Breakdown

(The following answers are only provided for guidance.)

A. Simple Sentence (p 106)

A-1 Abby is sledding down the hill right now.

A-2 Bobby and Dennis were eating in the cafeteria today.

A-3 I heard Lily wrote the cutest love letter to Samuel.

A-4 Wow, I didn't know that Ian folds laundry so well.

A-5 I can't believe Casey knows Chinese so fluently.

B. Compound Sentence (p 108)

B-1 Soccer is my favorite sport to play, but football is my favorite sport to watch.

B-2 Eating salad is one of the most healthiest options available, but pizza is much more tasty.

B-3 Black Sabbath plays great live shows, and Led Zeppelin plays pretty well, too.

B-4 The plush sofa sits in the middle of the room, and the patterned chair sits in the corner.

B-5 The gym is located near my house, and there is always an open treadmill to use.

C. Complex Sentence (p 110)

C-1 After working a long morning shift, I'm going to head home and enjoy my leftover apple pie and a fresh cup of coffee.

C-2 Despite constant quarreling, Kevin and Mindy remain best friends who do everything together.

C-3 The thick set of trees and bushes immediately appear through the narrow passageway.

C-4 The awards and prizes sit behind the curtain, hidden from curious viewers.

C-5 Before the invention of pens, typewriters, and computers, quill and ink were the only utensils used for writing.

D. Declarative, Exclamatory, Imperative, Interrogative (p 112)

D-1 exclamatory

D-2 interrogative

D-3 declarative

D-4 imperative

D-5 imperative

D-6 exclamatory

D-7 interrogative

D-8 declarative

D-9 imperative

D-10 exclamatory

Chapter 12. Punctuation, Common Phrasal Verbs, and Idioms

A. Punctuation (p 119)

A-1 period	**A-5** period	**A-8** exclamation point
A-2 exclamation point	**A-6** period	**A-9** exclamation point
A-3 period	**A-7** exclamation point	**A-10** period
A-4 exclamation point		

B. Colon or Semicolon (p 121)

B-1 colon	**B-5** colon	**B-8** semicolon
B-2 colon	**B-6** colon	**B-9** semicolon
B-3 semicolon	**B-7** semicolon	**B-10** semicolon
B-4 semicolon		

C. Parentheses (p 123)

C-1 Paulina (and Jack) are going to the new play tonight in downtown.

C-2 Zelda (also known as the crazy cat lady) adopted two more cats this morning

C-3 If you can get to the game on time (or even if you're late), please help out at the concessions stand for me.

C-4 What are you going to do with these wall decorations (or the window treatments) lying on the floor?

C-5 Other than staying up until 4 a.m. (and consuming way too much caffeine), the project turned out well!

C-6 Whether you go (or don't go), I will be there around 4 p.m. this afternoon.

C-7 Katie (also known as the dragon slayer) beats all her guy friends at video games.

C-8 I packed all the boxes (and maybe some other bags) in the car to take to the garage sale tomorrow morning.

C-9 During the latter portion of the exam, I think I messed up my answers (or maybe it was in the beginning).

C-10 Until an hour ago (or maybe it was earlier than that), I didn't know that I am the valedictorian of my class when we graduate!

D. Commas in Compound Sentence (p 126)

D-1 The lake isn't frozen enough for us to ice skate on, but we can go sledding down the hill instead.

D-2 I took cold medicine this morning, and I plan on taking more before I go to bed tonight.

D-3 Elle either went to the ballet practice this morning, or she went yesterday morning before school.

D-4 Take a spoonful of sugar, and sprinkle it over the entire batter.

D-5 Dean is the new mascot for the football team, and Annie is the new student coordinator.

D-6 You need to sign up for the SAT prep course, or you need to start studying on your own.

D-7 I'm excited for June's party because June's dad, who just got back from Afghanistan, will be there.

D-8 Have you heard U2's new music, or have you been finding other new music?

D-9 I'm ready to go to dinner, but are Daniel and Raquel ready?

D-10 When it comes to staying active, Taylor likes to run but John would rather lift weights.

E. Commas for Nonessential Words or Clauses (p 128)

E-1 Convinced that it wasn't a joke, Mrs. Curtis filed a complaint against the entire senior class because of their school prank.

E-2 In this case, however, I believe that Lionel has a right to be mad at you.

E-3 Quail, even though you don't understand it, is a delicacy in some countries.

E-4 Lastly, I believe that I should be accepted into your engineering program because I want to become aerospace engineer and work for NASA.

E-5 Kendall, the winner of the spelling bee for four years in a row, lost to Mindy this afternoon.

E-6 Daniel Radcliffe, known for his role as Harry Potter, is now starring in other movies in hopes to stop being associated with his first role.

E-7 Second, I would love to thank my mom and dad for supporting during high school.

E-8 Other than being the middle sister, Florence has always been overlooked in her family and at school.

E-9 Listen to your parents; otherwise, you may make a mistake that you can't take back.

E-10 Donald Trump, known for controversial behavior, is a great philanthropist who gives back to the community.

F. Quotation Marks **(p 131)**

F-1 The food reviewer of the new restaurant located in lower downtown said that the specialty dishes are "superb and fresh".

F-2 Have you ever read Dickens' "A Christmas Carol", "Our Mutual Friend", or "Oliver Twist"?

F-3 Please explain to grandma what "LOL" means.

F-4 My favorite plays by Shakespeare are "Hamlet", "Othello", "Romeo and Juliet", and "The Tempest".

F-5 Johnny, why do your guy friends call you "bro"?

F-6 According to the article in Woodfield Daily, the new park that just opened up is "safe for the kids, fun for the whole family, and a great place for a cookout".

F-7 In his poem "Bright Star", John Keats writes about his love for a girl named Fanny.

F-8 "God Bless America" isn't sung as much nowadays at baseball games or other sporting events.

F-9 Do you understand what's going on in "The Bell Jar" by Sylvia Plath?

F-10 Although you don't understand its meaning, calling someone a "bro" is a term of endearment.

G. Hyphens **(p 133)**

G-1 Hey! Stop that truck—

G-2 Can you please help me find my blue-green scarf to wear to dinner tonight?

G-3 My 11-year-old brother can do the neatest tricks.

G-4 Wait, I was just about to—

G-5 Please pick out your favorite clear-coated primer paint.

G-6 When you use *-ing*, it depicts that the word is showing present action.

G-7 Other than the other shirt I picked out, I think the grayish-white one looks best on you.

G-8 Gerald's hand-me-down shirts and pant look too big on his frame.

G-9 Until school is over, you need to keep up with day-to-day homework assignments.

G-10 I have no clue where this road is—

H. Apostrophe (p 136)

H-1 Please don't throw my old shows away.

H-2 Becky's twin sister attends Penn University.

H-3 The cat's food bowl was spilt everywhere when I got home. (hint: plural)

H-4 Ashlynn's diary is full of stupid stuff about boys and drama with girls.

H-5 Honey, have you seen Professor Judy's and Jim's research report around here?

H-6 Won't you consider studying a little harder for geography in the future?

H-7 Plenty of peoples' attention are distracted by social media lately. It's bad.

H-8 Underneath the windowsill, you'll find our mother's new pet.

H-9 Can't you study without the rest of your study group?

H-10 I couldn't be that nice to my sibling, if you'd ask me.

I. Slash, Bracket, or Dash (p 139)

I-1 slash	**I-5** slash	**I-8** bracket
I-2 bracket	**I-6** dash	**I-9** dash
I-3 bracket	**I-7** slash	**I-10** slash
I-4 bracket		

J. Verb Phrases (p 141)

J-1 Bring your water bottle over here to fill it up.

J-2 Drop your report off so I can read it over.

J-3 Let me point out some flaws in your original formula.

J-4 Put away your cellphone, Peter!

J-5 The teacher raised her voice to talk over the loud classroom.

J-6 Rhonda, hang up the laundry, please!

J-7 How long did it take you to set up your computer software?

J-8 I love to give back to my community.

J-9 I'm just put off by Suzy's snide comment earlier.

J-10 Will you look over my shoulder for a second?

K. Inseparable Phrasal Verbs (p 144)

K-1 Can I take over managing the project now?

K-2 Mrs. Briggs will look into other college options for her son.

K-3 I'm not here to wait on you hand and foot!

K-4 I told Oliver to call on me tomorrow afternoon.

K-5 Please go through these stacks of papers today.

K-6 Will you look after the newborn for me?

K-7 I think I saw the fawn run across the creek last night.

K-8 Jacob accidently ran into a tree while playing football.

K-9 I like to think I take after my grandfather.

K-10 Go over to Jill's house later.

L. Three-Word Phrasal Verbs (p 147)

L-1 I'm always afraid that a burglar is always going to break in on me.

L-2 I won't put up with your dirty habits any longer!

L-3 It's always good to look in on what your child is up to is his or her room.

L-4 Can't you keep up with me?

L-5 Get rid of those stinky shoes, please!

L-6 Can you make sure of this incident?

L-7 Take care of your grandmother for me while I'm gone.

L-8 Don't you get along with Janice and Jackie?

L-9 Let's catch up with our weekly TV show.

L-10 Look out for that falling tree!

M. Intransitive Phrasal Verbs (p 149)

M-1 You're such a show off, Jimmy!

M-2 Keep on down the road, and turn left.

M-3 Please slow down before I pass out.

M-4 I do some of my homework just to get by.

M-5 Pass on positivity, Sally!

M-6 Come back and eat some apple pie.

M-7 Eat out tonight if you feel like it.

M-8 When will Fanny ever catch on?

M-9 Can you come to gym class today?

M-10 Please come over next week for yoga!

Chapter 13. Sentence Fragments

A. Appositive Phrase (p 155)

A-1 Linda, the head of the school board, is excited to start her new term.

A-2 The owl that slept during the day was seen flying around at night.

A-3 Harry Potter, the boy who lived, ultimately defeated Lord Voldemort.

A-4 Pauline, who lived in Alaska for most of her life, wasn't used to the warm weather.

A-5 The box that's been on the shelf for so many years holds too many secrets to count.

A-6 Jenelle, the girl with a really good fast pitch, won the national championship game.

A-7 The fence that only I can jump over tripped Curtis the other day.

A-8 Diana, a Greek goddess, comforted mortals from time to time.

A-9 Lobsters that are caught in Maine taste the best!

A-10 The watercolor painting that was in the art museum was stolen over the weekend!

B. Subordinate Clauses (p 157)

B-1 We went to another restaurant even though the wait was almost over.

B-2 After everything was thoroughly finished, my dad smiled with pride.

B-3 Sassy the cat sleep behinds the tattered, velvet curtain.

B-4 During the beautiful wedding reception downtown, I danced the night away.

B-5 I'm okay, other than being embarrassed by the fall.

B-6 I buried myself beneath the blankets and covers because I was so cold.

B-7 I spilled ketchup onto the kitchen floor.

B-8 Before the quintet performance is my solo.

B-9 Under the tree where I read books, I found a family of raccoons sitting there.

B-10 There is a beautiful house situated between two hills.

C. Verb Phrase Sentence Fragments (p 160)

C-1 Last night I ate with my entire family and friends.

C-2 Johnny kept her journal since middle school by his night stand.

C-3 Kyle bought groceries down the street.

C-4 Jenny tried to taker her final exam early so she could visit her family.

C-5 I can't believe Kim juggled five balls at one time.

C-6 I can't seem to get all this paint off my clothes.

C-7 Aunt Helen baked cookies, a cake and brownies for the bake sale.

C-8 Rachel diced up some tomatoes for this recipe.

C-9 Professor Lionel knocked on the door to let them know he was there.

C-10 Derek dribbled the basketball like a pro athlete.

D. Infinitive Phrase Sentence Fragments (p 162)

D-1 How can I arrange the flowers in the prettiest manner?

D-2 I need to practice writing in the most succinct way.

D-3 I wish I could play guitar as good as my brother.

D-4 Katie will help make goodie bags for the homeless this holiday season.

D-5 The speaker will hand out prizes to the winners of the convention.

D-6 Let's get gas and start on our journey!

D-7 Please help me gather all the leaves into one pile.

D-8 The children wanted to hide from all the grownups in the house.

D-9 I can't wait to decorate the house for fall and Christmas!

D-10 When will we nominate the homecoming king and queen for this year?

E. Afterthought Sentence Fragments (p 164)

E-1 Just when I thought I was done with school for good, I decided to get my master's degree.

E-2 You could've done much better than I did on that test.

E-3 I'm probably just going to go to sleep now.

E-4 Lily would've gone to the baseball game instead of class.

E-5 I wish I had slept instead of staying up until 3 in the morning.

E-6 You just need to stop and take a deep breath.

E-7 Evan wishes he had a few A's rather than C's.

E-8 I can't believe Katie isn't coming to my graduation party.

E-9 My mother should've ordered my school uniform months ago instead of now.

E-10 Dylan tried to maneuver out of detention already.

F. Participle Phrase Sentence Fragments (p 167)

F-1 I tried pulling the long trailer behind the truck.

F-2 I'm figuring out if I want to go to band practice or not.

F-3 My parents are sailing from Florida to Maine this summer after school is out.

F-4 After wanting to go skiing in the Alps during Christmas break, Taylor booked us a trip!

F-5 The dogs are herding all the sheep into the pen once night falls.

F-6 Mrs. Fink hurt my feelings after circling all the wrong answers on my midterm test.

F-7 Studying for the SAT and ACT all summer long. I'm ready to take them.

F-8 Alan was elated for winning the state championship within the last quarter.

F-9 I kept busy knitting a couple of hats, scarves and mittens for my family.

F-10 Looking terrified from the amount of homework we were assigned, I left Natalie and Serena in despair.

Chapter 14. Dangling Modifiers

A. Dangling Modifiers (p 173)

A-1 The little girl was crying and ran over to her mom for comfort.

A-2 The teacher was dismayed and shook her head at the rambunctious classroom.

A-3 The skeptical lawyer was lying and walked briskly away from his client.

A-4 Candace, the last woman to leave the room, was tired and hurried home.

A-5 Manny, who faked a pass and won the game with a great run into the end zone, was elated.

A-6 Neither stubborn boy owned up to his mistake, so they stayed in time out.

A-7 Ewan was head over heels and wrote his girlfriend a love letter.

A-8 Even though he was dismayed, Lionel should still apologize even if he was in the right.

A-9 The old woman's death was tragic and a hard blow to everyone in the community.

A-10 Gwen, the newest dancer on the team, was excited and beamed brightly on the stage.

Chapter 15. Gerunds, Participles, and Idioms

A. Gerund (p 179)

A-1 swimming

A-2 cooking, panning

A-3 hunting

A-4 running, jumping

A-5 fencing

A-6 writing

A-7 hiking

A-8 biking

A-9 fishing

A-10 testing

B. Participle (p 182)

B-1 eating	**B-5** playing	**B-8** hasn't made
B-2 crying; holding	**B-6** deafening	**B-9** crinkling
B-3 diving; snorkeling	**B-7** doesn't miss	**B-10** head
B-4 sleeping		

C. Idiom (p 184)

C-1 a day late and a dollar short	**C-6** Break a leg
C-2 bit off more than she could chew	**C-7** Heat of the moment
C-3 cry me a river	**C-8** Make a long story short
C-4 Elvis has left the building	**C-9** Taste of her own medicine
C-5 Feeling under the weather	**C-10** Your guess is as good as mine

D. Create Your Own Sentences with Given Idioms (p 185)

D-1 I wouldn't be caught dead with you.

D-2 Take it with a grain of salt, honey.

D-3 Speak of the devil, here is Ernie!

D-4 Let's see eye to eye on this.

D-5 I think this assignment is a piece of cake.

D-6 I think you see the world through rose-colored glasses.

D-7 There is a method to my madness, I tell you!

D-8 You can't teach an old dog new tricks, Lois.

D-9 Are you keeping something at bay?

D-10 It takes two to tango, Freddie.

Chapter 16. Diction/Word Choice

A. Formal Diction Sentence (p 193)

A-1 Kyle, why did you hurt Kelsey's bike?

A-2 Oh my goodness. Can you believe Stacie?

A-3 Harry Potter is my favorite book series of all time.

A-4 Can you calm down?

A-5 Wow, my mother is terrific!

A-6 After I get out from work, let's meet up.

A-7 Isn't that the greatest?

A-8 Settle down, Joshua.

A-9 William and Jake are very handsome, don't you think?

A-10 Let me grab my belongings before we leave.

B. Formal Diction (p 195)

B-1 Yes	**B-5** Yes	**B-8** Yes
B-2 No	**B-6** Yes	**B-9** No
B-3 Yes	**B-7** No	**B-10** Yes
B-4 No		

C. Informal Diction (p 197)

C-1 Oliver tied the tire swing to the oak tree,

C-2 Regina loves using quills when writing.

C-3 The lions are sleeping in the shade.

C-4 Unlike Hayley, Dean hits the target every time with arrows

C-5 I went to Ghan on a missions trip to play with children.

C-6 Warren and Regina are eating downtown tonight.

C-7 The mama bear was protecting her cubs while they slept.

C-8 Jack loves playing with his Yo-Yo.

C-9 Harold runs quickly from his pet dog.

C-10 The squirrel hides nuts in the tree.

D. Informal Diction **(p 199)**

D-1 No	**D-5** No	**D-8** No
D-2 No	**D-6** No	**D-9** No
D-3 Yes	**D-7** Yes	**D-10** No
D-4 Yes		

E. Slang (also known as colloquialism) **(p 201)**

E-1 I don't know. Let me check my planner and see if I have next Friday off.

E-2 Wow, that new CD release from Beyonce is great!

E-3 Other than that, the new girl in our chemistry class seems average.

E-4 Did you see Roy snort milk out of his nose? I can't even believe that.

E-5 Unlike Patrick, this new boy over here is a great waiter.

E-6 Please let me know if you'll be able to make it to Easter dinner next week.

E-7 I always rely on my significant other to cheer me up after a bad day.

E-8 I need to go to bed now. Talk to you later!

E-9 To be honest, I prefer wearing jeans to work rather than dresses and dress pants.

E-10 How am I supposed to pass this class with my D average?

Chapter 17. Active and Passive Voice

A. Passive Voice to Active Voice (p 208)

A-1 Jackie marks the book with highlighters.

A-2 A mother raccoon from the woods stole Sam's backpack.

A-3 Samantha dropped a can of beans

A-4 Two little girls picked acorns under the tree.

A-5 Ben ate the cake on a sunny day.

A-6 Jane dropped a tub of chocolate ice cream, and it fell down the hill.

A-7 Robert's hands were quivering from fear, and he dropped them on the stage.

A-8 A plane dropped rescue packages down to mountain climbers just over the mountain.

A-9 Kenny's shotgun was heard in the distance.

A-10 Walter tripped and spilled a bowl of rice on the ground.

B. Active Voice (p 212)

B-1 Jill canned beets yesterday.

B-2 The twins laughed due to a joke they found from a book.

B-3 In "The Odyssey", you can read about Ajax and Hector.

B-4 The professor taught British Literature last semester.

B-5 Bill and Jan ate ice cream in the afternoon.

B-6 The fat cat sat underneath the table.

B-7 In the morning, Zachary and Ian kicked the soccer ball.

B-8 The kitten quivered from terror between the couch.

B-9 Carrie ran on the track in the afternoon.

B-10 Kyle rode his bike in the neighborhood.

C. Active or Passive Voice (p 214)

C-1 passive	**C-5** active	**C-8** passive
C-2 active	**C-6** active	**C-9** active
C-3 active	**C-7** active	**C-10** active
C-4 passive		

Chapter 18. Parallel Structure

A. Parallel Structure Rule 1 Sentences **(p 219)**

A-1 Jaime plays the trumpet in the band.
A-2 Benjamin Franklin writes a letter with a quill and sends it off.
A-3 But the dog is in the swimming pool!
A-4 Rachel and her sister went diving on a sunny day.
A-5 On the other hand, Lena drew a rainbow and tree very well.
A-6 Sammy and his dog, Paul, ran in the park.
A-7 Behind the couch, the rabbit slept on Sunday morning.
A-8 Xavier plays Pokemon on his Gameboy.
A-9 Evan loves doing yoga in his backyard.
A-10 Wendy and her boyfriend fence in the auditorium.

B. Parallel Structure Rule 1 **(p 222)**

B-1 Yes	**B-5** Yes	**B-8** Yes
B-2 No	**B-6** No	**B-9** No
B-3 Yes	**B-7** Yes	**B-10** Yes
B-4 Yes		

C. Parallel Structure Rule 2 Sentences **(p 223)**

C-1 Can you peel the potatoes, scrub the floor, and take out the trash for me?
C-2 Do you suggest switching math classes, taking AP history and finishing yearbook class?
C-3 After swimming, George also loves biking and rowing.
C-4 Quickly take this food to Aunt Millie's house and bake the rest of these cookies there.
C-5 Other than that, the test was simple and flew by quickly.
C-6 Anderson wanted to stir the soup while he talked to Pam on the phone.
C-7 In order to fix the bike, Jenny drove to the nearest store.
C-8 To be great at running and jumping hurdles, you must practice every day.
C-9 Derek is the leading rebounder and shooter on the basketball team.
C-10 Just because I'm shorter and wider than you doesn't mean I'm not as beautiful as you.

D. Parallel Structure Rule 2 (p 227)

D-1 I think the contestants on *American Idol* are awesome, hilarious, and talented.

D-2 Brent loves playing rugby because it's competitive, exhilarating, and rough.

D-3 Even though it's freezing out, muddy, and raining, I still love hiking during this time of year.

D-4 Either he's too busy doesn't know what's going on or just isn't interested in helping us out today.

D-5 Can we decide whether we are going to France, Italy, or Spain for vacation this summer?

D-6 When will Hannah finish the laundry, her homework, and go to ballet practice?

D-7 Quickly take the casserole out, set the table, and pour drinks for our guests.

D-8 Over the hill, through the woods ,and under the bridge is where Mr. Toad's house is.

D-9 In the evening I'm taking Katie, Emma, and Christie to their dance recital.

D-10 Andrea took James' backpack, calculator, and pencils to his exam for him

E. Parallel Structure Rule 3 (p 228)

E-1	False	**E-5**	True	**E-8**	False
E-2	True	**E-6**	True	**E-9**	False
E-3	True	**E-7**	True	**E-10**	True
E-4	True				

F. Parallel Structure Rule 4 (p 230)

F-1 Ophelia makes her dog practice sitting, but she doesn't do it well.

F-2 George enjoyed winning the trophy and receiving praise.

F-3 So the three brothers climbed the gorge.

F-4 Ian also eats peanut butter and jelly sandwiches.

F-5 Because he loves adventure, Dan enjoys cliff kayaking and skydiving.

F-6 Jackie made banana pudding then homemade chocolate.

F-7 Out of all the seasons, summer and winter are my favorite.

F-8 I am cooking and cleaning the rest of the day, so I can't go.

F-9 But I told Sally I'd go to the park and fly the kite with her.

F-10 I helped Yolanda with reading, writing and editing because I promised her last week.

Chapter 19. Transitional Devices

A. Transitional Devices (p 239)

A-1 For instance	**A-5** Naturally	**A-8** As stated
A-2 In contrast	**A-6** In fact	**A-9** In addition
A-3 As a result	**A-7** Yet	**A-10** Evidently
A-4 Obviously		

B. Sentences Using Transitional Devices (p 240)

B-1 Once in a while, Jane reads anime books for fun.

B-2 To demonstrate their skills, the two girls love to show off in hopscotch.

B-3 Since the season ended, my running shoes are worn out.

B-4 Sometimes, Derek lays over the couch.

B-5 Quail eggs are a delicacy in some countries, indeed.

B-6 In fact, jogging hurts my knees.

B-7 On the contrary, you kicked Peter during dodgeball.

B-8 Technically, Sam went to the movies around 3 p.m.

B-9 I can't go skiing in Aspen, as a result.

B-10 Moreover, jaguars are the fastest animals!

Chapter 20. Sentence Clarity

A. Sentence Clarity Question #1 (p 248)

A-1 Wordy		**A-5** Concise		**A-8** Concise	
A-2 Wordy		**A-6** Concise		**A-9** Wordy	
A-3 Wordy		**A-7** Concise		**A-10** Concise	
A-4 Concise					

B. Sentence Clarity Question #2 (p 250)

B-1 No		**B-5** No		**B-8** Yes	
B-2 No		**B-6** Yes		**B-9** No	
B-3 No		**B-7** No		**B-10** No	
B-4 Yes					

C. Sentence Clarity Question #3 (p 251)

C-1 Missing a verb		**C-5** Correct		**C-8** Correct	
C-2 Dangling modifier		**C-6** Missing a predicate		**C-9** Correct	
C-3 Dangling modifier		**C-7** Missing a subject		**C-10** Correct	
C-4 Dangling modifier					

D. Sentence Clarity Question #4 (p 254)

D-1 Yes		**D-5** Yes		**D-8** Yes	
D-2 No		**D-6** Yes		**D-9** Yes	
D-3 Yes		**D-7** Yes		**D-10** Yes	
D-4 Yes					

E. Sentence Clarity Question #5 (p 256)

E-1 No		**E-5** No		**E-8** Yes	
E-2 No		**E-6** Yes		**E-9** Yes	
E-3 Yes		**E-7** No		**E-10** No	
E-4 No					

GLOSSARY OF TERMS

This section compiles all the terms used throughout this book. Use it as a quick reference when you want to go over a difficult term or brush up on as a review.

Abstract Nouns: are ideas, characteristics, or qualities, such as courage, joy, love, peace, and ambition

Action Verbs: verbs that specifically describe what the subject of the sentence is acting out. These types of verbs demonstrate information in a sentence, sometimes convey different emotions, and a sense of purpose that extends beyond the literal meanings of the words.

Active Voice: the subject participates in the action; most writing should be written in active voice (passive voice is considered poor writing)

Adjectives: a word or phrase naming an attribute, added to or grammatically related to a noun to modify or describe it.

Adverbs: a word or phrase that modifies or qualifies an adjective, verb, or other adverb or a word group, expressing a relation of place, time, circumstance, manner, cause, or degree

Antecedent: the word for which the pronoun stands (i.e. Bill – noun; he – pronoun)

Appositives: a noun, noun phrase, or series of nouns placed next to another word or phrase to identify or rename it.

Articles: a particular item or object, typically one of a specified type.

Base Form: basic form of a verb before conjugation into tenses

Comparative Forms: compare two or more things or persons

Complement: part of a sentence that completes or adds meaning to the predicate

Compound Sentence: sentence with at least two independent clauses; usually joined by a conjunction

Coordinating Conjunctions: a conjunction placed between words, phrases, clauses, or sentences of equal rank, such as *and, but,* and *or*

Dangling Participle: illogical structure that occurs in a sentence when a writer intends to modify one thing but the reader attaches it to another

Declarative Sentence: sentences that usually make a simple statement

Dependent Clauses: a clause that is always used as some part of speech. It can be an adjective, adverb, or noun and cannot stand alone as a sentence.

Direct Object: receives the action by the subject

Elliptical Clauses: an adverb clause that uses *than* and *as* to introduce the clause. i.e. You are prettier *than* she. They always modify the comparative word.

Exclamation Point: a punctuation mark used to express a strong feeling, such as happiness, anger, surprise, or incredulity

Fragment: incomplete piece of a sentence used alone as a complete sentence; a fragment does not contain a complete thought; fragments are common in normal speech but unusual (inappropriate) in formal writing

Genitive Case: case expressing relationship between nouns (possession, origin, composition etc.)

Gerunds: a verbal that always ends in *-ing* and is used as a noun. i.e. *Running is fun.* It can be a subject, direct object, predicate nominative, appositive, indirect object, or object of a preposition.

Imperative Sentence: a sentence that makes a command or request

Independent Clause: group of words that expresses a complete thought and can stand alone as a sentence

Interrogative Pronouns: ask questions; they include *who, whom, which, what* etc.

Irregular Verbs: a verb in which the past tense is not formed by adding the usual -ed ending.

Mood: sentence type that indicates the speaker's view towards the degree of reality of what is being said, for example subjunctive, indicative, imperative

Nouns: a word (other than a pronoun) used to identify any of a class of people, places, or things common noun, or to name a particular one of these proper noun.

Objective pronouns: a personal **pronoun** that is used typically as a grammatical **object**: the direct or indirect **object** of a verb, or the **object** of a preposition. **Object pronouns** contrast with subject **pronouns**.

Participle: verb form that can be used as an adjective or a noun

Passive Voice: is a grammatical construction (specifically, a "**voice**"). The noun or noun phrase that would be the object of an active sentence (such as Our troops defeated the enemy) appears as the subject of a sentence with **passive voice.**

Past Participle: verb form; usually made by adding *-ed* to the base verb; typically used in perfect and passive tenses, and sometimes as an adjective

Past Perfect: tense that refers to the past in the past (had + *verb*-ed)

Period: a punctuation mark used at the end of the sentence

Plural Form: indicating more than one person or thing

Predicate Nominative: a word that completes a linking verb and renames the subject

Prepositions: a word governing, and usually preceding, a noun or pronoun and expressing a relation to another word or element in the clause

Prepositional Phrase: a modifying phrase consisting of a preposition and its object.

Pronouns: a word that can function by itself as a noun phrase and that refers either to the participants in the discourse or to someone or something mentioned elsewhere in the discourse

Pronoun-Antecedent Agreement: The **pronoun** must **agree** with its **antecedent** in number. Rule: A singular **pronoun** must replace a singular noun; a plural **pronoun** must replace a plural noun.

Punctuation: the marks, such as period, comma, and parentheses, used in writing to separate sentences and their elements and to clarify meaning.

Qualifiers: are adverbs that strengthen or weaken the words they modify

Relative Pronouns: that introduce a restrictive **relative** clause aren't separated from the main clause by a comma. Restrictive **relative** clauses (also known as **defining relative** clauses) add essential information about the antecedent in the main clause.

Sentence: a group of words expressing a complete thought, and it must have a *subject* and a *verb*

Subject: a word that tells who or what about the verb

Subjective Pronouns: is a personal **pronoun** that is used as the subject of a verb. Subject **pronouns** are usually in the nominative case for languages with a nominative–accusative alignment pattern. In English the subject **pronouns** are I, you, he, she, it, we, they, what, and who.

Subject-verb Agreement: means the **subject** and **verb** must **agree** in number. This **means** both need to be singular or both need to be plural.

Superlative Forms: compares more than two things or persons. i.e. oldest, loveliest, highest

Syntax: sentence structure

Verbs: a word used to describe an action, state, or occurrence, and forming the main part of the predicate of a sentence, such as *hear, become, happen.*

Verb Tenses: is the form of the **verb** that indicates time. A verb tense not only indicates past, present, and future action, but also indicates whether the action is ongoing or complete.

Voice: form of a verb that shows the relation of the subject to the action

VOCABULARY TERMS (AND MORE)

One of the most helpful ways of becoming a strong writer is learning to use strong vocabulary words and active verbs in your writing. Below are some vocabulary words and active verbs. Feel free to make flashcards and start using them in your everyday conversation and writing. You will improve your diction, as well as impress others.

Abate: (v.) to reduce in amount, degree, or severity

Abbreviate: (v.) to shorten, abridge

Abhor: (v.) to hate

Accord (v.) concurrence of opinion

Advocate: (v.) to speak favor of

Aesthetic: (adj.) concerning the appreciation of beauty

Amicable: (adj.) friendly, agreeable

Anachronistic: (adj.) not attributed to the correct historical period

Anecdote: (n.) short account of an event, story

Anomaly: (n.) deviation from what is normal

Apathy: (n.) lack of interest or emotion

Assiduous: (adj.) persistent, hard-working

Banal: (adj.) boring, clichéd

Benevolent: (adj.) friendly, helpful

Candid: (adj.) impartial and honest (especially in speech)

Chaos: (n.) great disorder or confusion

Condone: (v.) to overlook, pardon, or disregard

Counterfeit: (v.) fake; false

Covert: (v. or n.) hidden; undercover

Cower: (v) to recoil in fear or servility; shrink away from

Credible: (adj.) believable

Credulous: (adj.) gullible; ready to believe anything

Decorum: (n.) appropriate behavior or conduct; propriety

Deride: (v.) to speak of or treat with contempt; to mock or belittle

Dilate: (v.) to expand or make larger

Discern: (v.) to recognize or perceive

Dogmatic: (v.) one's firm opinions or beliefs

Eminent (adj.): high in a position, merit or esteem

Emphatic: (adj.): spoken with special impressiveness

Emulate (v.): to imitate with intent to equal or surpass

Encumber (v.) to impede with obstacles

Enigma: (n.) puzzle; mystery

Enmity (n.): hatred

Ensnare (v.): to entrap

Entail (v.): to involve; necessitate

Enthuse (v.): to yield to or display intense emotion

Entirety (n.): a complete thing

Exasperate (v.): to excite great anger in

Facetious (adj.): amusing

Fallacious (adj.): illogical

Feasible (adj.): an action that may be done, performed or effected

Fervid (adj.): intense

Finite (adj.): limited

Furtherance (n.): advancement

Gaiety (n.): festivity

Galore (adj.): abundant

Garrulous (adj.): given to constant trivial talking

Generality (n.): the principal portion

Ghastly (adj.): hideous

Gradient (adj.): moving or advancing by steps

Gumption (n.): common sense

Halcyon (adj.): calm

Harangue (n.): tirade

Heedless (adj.): thoughtless

Hereditary (adj.): passing from parent to child

Hinder (v.): to obstruct

Hoard (v.): to gather and store away for the sake of accumulation

Humanize (v.): to make gentle or refined

Icon (n.): an image or likeness

Iconoclastic (v.): against the norm

Illusive (adj.): deceptive

Immaculate (adj.): without spot or blemish

Imminence (n.): impending danger or evil

Jargon (n.): confused, unintelligible speech or highly technical speech

Jocular (adj.): inclined to joke

Juxtapose (adj.): to contrast two objects

Knavery (n.): deceit

Labyrinth (n.): a maze

Laud (v.): to praise

Lethargic (adj.): lazy, sluggish

Lenient (adj.): to be merciful

Liable (adj.): justly or legally responsible

Libel (n.): defamation

Lithe (adj.): supple

Magnitude (n.): importance

Maleficent (adj.): mischievous

Mandate (n.): command

Maxim (n.): a principle accepted as true and acted on as a rule or guide

Meager (adj.): little

Mendacious (adj.): a lie

Nefarious (adj.): wicked in the extreme

Negate (v.): to deny

Nestle (adj.): to be cozily situated

Obnoxious (adj.): odious; not liked

Observant (adj.): quick to notice

Obstruction (n.): hindrance

Omniscience (n.): all-knowing

Pagan (n.): worshipper of false gods

Palatial (adj.): magnificent

Paradox (n.): a contradicted statement

Pariah (n.): social outcast

Petulant (adj.): displaying impatience

Poise (n.): balance

Protrusion (n.): sticking out

Quarrelsome (adj.): irritable

Query (v.): to make an inquiry

Quixotic (adj.): chivalrous; romantic in notions

Recessive (adj.): having a tendency to go back

Reciprocal (v.): mutually interchangeable

Reckless (adj.): heedless of danger

Rectify (v.): to correct

Redolent (adj.): smelling sweet and agreeable

Relent (v.): to yield

Retort (n.): retaliating speech

Salutary (adj.): beneficial

Sanctify (v.): to purify; make clean

Sonorous (adj.): pleasant-sounding

Specious (adj.): plausible

Stagnation (n.): the condition of not flowing or moving

Tacit (adj.): understood

Tenacious (adj.): perseverance

Terse (adj.): pithy

Tirade (n.): ranting speech

Tranquil (adj.): calm; peaceful

Unanimous (adj.): sharing the same views or emotions

Usage (n.): treatment

Vacate (v.): to leave

Vacuous (adj.): empty

Venerate (v.): to cherish

Verify (v.): to prove true

Wantonness (n.): reckless

Wiry (adj.): thin but tough

Writhe (v.): to twist in pain

Zenith (n.): prosperity or greatness

Action Verbs

Action verbs make a huge difference in your writing style. They add a powerful effect to sentences and eliminate useless verbiage. Below are just a few of the best active verbs to use. Practice using them in speech or written communication. You'll notice how sentences will become stronger and improve your tone immensely.

Accelerate	Balance	Contact	Devise
Accomplish	Boost	Contribute	Devote
Achieve	Brief	Control	Differentiate
Acquire	Broaden	Convince	Direct
Adapt	Build	Coordinate	Discuss
Add	Calculate	Cultivate	Distinguish
Address	Capture	Debate	Earn
Adjust	Catalog	Decide	Edit
Advise	Categorize	Decrease	Effect
Align	Charge	Dedicate	Enforce
Allocate	Check	Deduce	Enhance
Amend	Clarify	Defend	Entertain
Analyze	Cooperate	Defer	Equip
Answer	Collaborate	Define	Estimate
Anticipate	Collect	Delegate	Expedite
Apply	Communicate	Deliver	Extend
Approve	Compile	Demonstrate	Fabricate
Arrange	Compose	Depict	Facilitate
Assemble	Conceptualize	Derive	Finalize
Assist	Conclude	Describe	Formulate
Attend	Condense	Design	Foster
Attract	Confirm	Determine	Frame
Award	Construct	Develop	Gather

Generate	Master	Recognize	Substitute
Grant	Maximize	Recreate	Stimulate
Guide	Mediate	Reduce	Strategize
Handle	Mentor	Reference	Surpass
Illustrate	Minimize	Regulate	Sustain
Impart	Modify	Relate	Symbolize
Implement	Monitor	Renew	Tend
Incorporate	Motivate	Resolve	Trace
Influence	Narrate	Restore	Transcribe
Initiate	Navigate	Retain	Transfer
Innovate	Notify	Retrieve	Translate
Insure	Observe	Revamp	Unify
Integrate	Obtain	Reveal	Update
Intervene	Operate	Revise	Utilize
Investigate	Perceive	Revitalize	Validate
Justify	Perform	Secure	Value
Launch	Prevent	Serve	Verify
Liquidate	Project	Settle	View
Litigate	Promote	Simplify	Vitalize
Localize	Propose	Simulate	Withdraw
Maintain	Publish	Solve	Witness
Manage	Qualify	Strength	Yield
Market	Quantify	Substantiate	

ADDITIONAL RESOURCES

Below are additional resources for learning better writing habits. Feel free to explore these different websites and links that will make your writing better and stronger.

- Purdue OWL: https://owl.english.purdue.edu/owl/

- The University of Chicago Writing Program: http://writing-program. uchicago.edu/resources/grammar.htm

- The Blue Book of Grammar and Punctuation: http://www.grammarbook. com/

- The Center for Writing Studies (the University of Illinois at Urbana-Champaign: http://www.cws.illinois.edu/workshop/writers/

- Grammar Practice Sheets (ASU College of Liberal Arts & Sciences): http://english.clas.asu.edu/enged-grammarpractice

- Vocabulary Lists: http://www.majortests.com/word-lists/

- Houghton Mifflin Books' Top 100 Vocabulary Words: http://www. houghtonmifflinbooks.com/booksellers/press_release/100words/

- Additional Grammar Worksheets (Baton Rouge Community College): http://guides.mybrcc.edu/grammarworksheets

- Grammarbook.com

BIBLIOGRAPHY

List of Action Verbs (Harvard Law School): http://www.law.harvard.edu/current/careers/opia/toolkit/resumes/action-verbs.html

Daily Grammar: http://www.dailygrammar.com/glossary.html

English Club: https://www.englishclub.com/grammar/terms.htm

INDEX